A Wee I

Published by David J Publishing 2015
Copyright © 2015 by Kenneth Patterson

First David J Publishing edition 2015
www.davidjpublishing.com

Cover Design: Jacqueline Stokes

A CIP catalogue record for this book is available from the British Library
ISBN: 978-0-9934591-1-5

Also by Kenneth Patterson

Says You Says I

Acknowledgements

This work is a sequel to my first book, *Says You, Says I: A Belfast Childhood*, which was written following my son's suggestions for recording these memories after hearing my tales of my childhood in Belfast.

A Wee Dander narrates my experiences after leaving my Belfast home and broadening my horizons in the Merchant Navy. Thanks must go once again to my son for his persistence and encouragement in the writing of this second work.

I must also thank my wife, Mary, as always for putting up with my impatience.

Last, but certainly not least, David Stokes of David J Publishing, who published my first book and has kindly decided to publish my second work.

Many thanks to all

Dedication

For Mary, Tara and Craig

A Wee Dander

by

Kenneth Patterson

DAVID J
PUBLISHING

Breaks my heart to see you live this way,
Scared of everything, every single day.
I can't sit still: too much in my head.
I got to break out of this place somehow,
While I'm still young and alive.

I'll go walking down to Sailortown,
And I'll look out to sea.
When them big ships come sailing in,
Maybe this one's for me...
'Sailortown' by Energy Orchard

Chapter One

Almost There

TO MY SURPRISE, joining the Merchant Navy turned out to be straightforward and uneventful. Like so many events that change our lives, it happened without incident. This smooth transition came about because at the time my oldest sister was stepping out with a chap called Tommy McGee. Along with his Da, Tommy crewed one of the many tugboats which guided ships into and out of the port of Belfast. This of course meant that over the years Tommy came into contact with ships' crews and port workers. He would become my fixer on more than one occasion.

Tommy and I had talked about the Merchant Navy for months and he knew how keen I was to join, if the opportunity arose. One day, Tommy informed me that he had made arrangements to introduce me to a chap who was employed at the docks. I never did learn Bobby's surname, but he told me that he worked as a checker. Part of his duties was to record ingoing and outgoing ships' cargoes and he was quite influential with ships' officers and port authorities. Bobby talked to someone on board ship who talked to someone else who brought Tommy and me on board to meet the Chief Steward. He was very smartly dressed in his uniform, and in my naïve eyes I thought he was the captain of the ship; he was in fact in charge of the catering department. I met this man with enthusiasm and shook hands; he then informed me that I could join the ship in a week's time if I wanted to. My entry into the Merchant Navy was, to say the least, painless, although my exit was to be quite different...

What I did learn, a few weeks after joining the ship The Duke of Rothesay, was that the requirement for entering the Merchant navy was to undergo a three–month training course, and the minimum age on entry was sixteen years and three months. If this information was correct, which I believe it was, then I had definitely, at the tender age of fifteen years and some months (and with the help of Tommy and Bobby) escaped this ritual. Nepotism, I was to learn through the years, can sometimes be a very powerful tool.

The Duke of Rothesay

Within just a few weeks, I would be stepping onto my first gangplank and boarding my first ship, The Duke of Rothesay, in the port of Belfast.

Because of the training I had received as a commis chef at the prestigious Grand Central Hotel (during a brief stay of about a year), the Chief Steward informed me that I would be employed as a member of the catering staff. Specifically, my duties would be in

10

the galley: washing pots and pans and cooking utensils, mopping the galley deck and generally keeping the place clean. But I would also be encouraged to look and learn when I had a break, and so eventually become a chef. This I did with gusto, and over the ensuing months I would learn the basics of cooking and how the ship's cooks went about their business. My previous training in The Grand Central Hotel was to stand me in good stead.

Although I had a week to go before I would join the ship, the Chief Steward suggested that I should come down in the early evening and meet two of the cooks with whom I would be working. That evening I was introduced to Tommy Burke, the chef, and George, or as I was to discover later, Old George as he was exclusively known. Apt I would say, because to my young eyes Old George looked as though he was ready for the knackers' yard. Old George did a bit of cooking, but apart from that, I never did find out what his position was. 'Assistant Cook' would be an appropriate job description for the old boy.

Tommy Burke was a man of approximately six feet two inches tall. A slim but well–muscled man: not an inch of fat clung to his frame. Tommy, I discovered in that brief time we met, was a man of few words. He was certainly not rude, spoke when he was spoken to and rationed his words. Because of this he appeared somewhat aloof to me at first, but after I had been on board the ship a few weeks, I would learn that Tommy was a hundred per cent okay. He would take me under his wing and turn out to be a good friend; he would also come to be my bodyguard and protector.

There was a third cook: his name was Joe Burns. He would be joining the ship later that evening, so I would meet him a week later when I came on board. He was the second cook, and he liked to be known as 'Chef'. Joe lived in Larne a few miles outside Belfast. The arrangement was that Tommy would be the duty cook departing Belfast, and Joe would be the duty cook leaving the port of Heysham.

As for Old George, he would be on duty whenever it suited him, although he seemed to be in the galley all of the time. He was a character that this young man had never encountered before. I shook hands with the old fellow and I could not believe my eyes:

there he was standing before me. To describe him as 'dishevelled' would be an understatement: a tramp was natty compared to Old George. He was wearing an old pair of stained cook's trousers; they fitted where they touched. A tattered pair of house slippers and a dirty old cardigan, well aired, with a few holes here and there.

To my disbelief, this was the way Old George would always appear for duty in the galley: hygiene at its zenith. Old George always had a smile on his face; he was beaming from ear to ear, but this did not disguise the fact that to me he looked ninety years of age, which of course he was not, although he was well past retirement age. The understanding was most likely that if he did not collapse or falter, he could stay on board. A Merchant Navy form of Welfare State, looking after its own. Somewhere between an Assistant Cook and general dogsbody, he did do his share of cooking, and whatever his position was, it did not matter to this young man. He made me feel at home immediately, knowing that this was a whole new world to me. He made me feel as if we had known each other for years instead of being comparative strangers, which is what we actually were. That is a rare gift for any human being, whether a scruffy dogsbody, prince or millionaire. This meant a lot to me, and Old George and I would become good friends. He always had that smile on his face, a sunny disposition, and he would always make me laugh with his not infrequently dirty jokes.

Joe Burns on the other hand, would turn out to be a different proposition, a right little sweetheart... But that was a future which had not yet happened, and I left the ship that evening with a spring in my step, stealing back into the darkening streets of Belfast where I would linger for not much longer.

In a few weeks' time I would be embarking on a completely new way of life, completely different to everything I had known up to that point in time: 1959. No doubt about that...

Chapter Two

Standing at the Corner

THE JOURNEY FROM the Belfast docks to my house took about thirty minutes on foot and I had a smile on my face all the way home. For once in my life, I felt no apprehension whatsoever.

In the next few days I would buy or borrow a holdall; my Ma would wash and iron my clothes and turn me out smart. I would tell some of my cousins, aunts, uncles and friends my news. A couple of my chums and I would go on a couple of long walks, which we often did, and end up back at our favourite spot, Lynch's pub. We would then proceed to look at the pretty girls passing by on their way along the Antrim Road. Standing on the corner watching all the girls go by was a wonderful occupation which I often recalled from the other side of the world with fondness, nostalgia and longing…

My pals and I would stand outside Lynch's pub, especially on those long, balmy summer evenings, and whistle at the girls dressed in their summer finery. Sometimes, to our surprise, they would look back at us and smile, and that little gesture was all the encouragement we needed. We would then really push our luck, catch up with the girls and walk alongside them, engage in conversation, and perhaps walk them to their door; and if we were really lucky they would agree to meet us again for a date. Mind you, that was a rare occurrence and we felt incredibly blessed if they said 'yes'. On that first date, with a peck on the cheek, or a light brush of lips, we were on cloud nine. We were an innocent and naïve lot.

Lynch's pub was our meeting place; it stood on the top of the New Lodge Road, adjacent to the Antrim Road. Singleton Street, where I lived and where I had grown up in the late 1940s and 50s, was two streets down from the pub. Yes, Lynch's pub is where we all assembled; the young lads would talk about the girls or what film was showing at the Lyceum Picture House, which stood opposite the pub on the top of the New Lodge Road.

The Lyceum Picture House

The older boys or men would be talking about football, cricket, or would be putting the world to rights; and of course, they would be discussing girls. How were we to know that a few short years later all this would change? The stories that the older ones told, all the jokes we enjoyed, all the laughter that reverberated around our corner pub, would disappear forever when the guns came out. Our assembly point, our meeting place, would vanish,

14

would be no more, when all along we had thought that it would last forever.

The troubles in Northern Ireland started around about 1968 and went on for about thirty years. Some people and some areas really felt the pain more than others, but everyone and every district were affected. The New Lodge Road area, where I spent my childhood and part of my teens, suddenly became the most dangerous place to live in Northern Ireland. That particular place took more than its share of the brunt of the war that raged between the different religions and the different terrorist gangs. That corner of the New Lodge Road at Lynch's pub opposite the Lyceum picture house was, at one point, statistically the most dangerous spot at which to stand in Northern Ireland.

A dangerous place to be during the Troubles

This little inconspicuous area, which had once been the centre of our little world, was vulnerable to paramilitaries throughout the troubles and particularly to drive–by shootings. A few short years earlier my friends and I had stood there outside the pub. We had argued, debated, laughed, whistled and smiled at the pretty girls walking by, without a care in the world. The contrast between those two times haunts me to this day.

None of us ever imagined, especially on those long carefree summer days, that a virtual civil war would erupt again on this beautiful green island, and that lives would be disrupted, destroyed and made to vanish away. Death and destruction could have been avoided by politicians sitting round a table and talking to all parties concerned for as long as was needed. By give and take, as all problems and conflicts wherever they may be are resolved. The violence never achieved a single thing: history has shown us that. In a democracy there will always be disagreements, demonstrations and discord, but as long as there is compromise and foresight these problems can eventually be resolved, and they will be resolved one way or the other. Violence just perpetuated the problem, as well as causing profound unhappiness and tragedy on an untold scale.

Today optimism shines through in Northern Ireland and peace prevails. Peace has won the war.

Years later, Lynch's pub got a make-over. Today, it no longer exists.

Chapter Three

On My Way

A **WEEK LATER** I was saying goodbye to Ma and Da and the family. There were no tears of sadness that I could see in anyone's eyes; if I had looked closer, I probably would have detected tears of relief. With my departure, there would be more room in the house, less congestion in the bedrooms and less competition for food. I got on well with my siblings; Freddie, the eldest, kept Albert and I in check. My sisters of course were my favourites, with Albert being my partner in crime.

How could there be tears? I wasn't going to spend months circumnavigating the globe: I would be home every other day. Eventually I would go deep sea but not for a couple of years yet.

Early that evening I went on board the Duke of Rothesay for the second time; this time I would be a member of the crew. I was met by the Purser who directed me to my cabin, which was quite roomy. It had a sink, two small wardrobes, a cabinet with two sets of drawers and two bunk beds. No bath or shower, as they were communal. I would occupy the top bunk and Tommy Burke the bottom bunk.

I stowed my kit away, and proceeded to make my way

along the passageway, up a set of stairs, along another small passageway, and entered the galley. I was met by Tommy Burke and Old George.

Tommy told me to look around the galley and familiarise with the layout. As I did, a very fat man approached me from out of nowhere. He was wearing a cheap suit, had a cigarette in one hand and a mug of tea in the other hand. He started to address me in a very abrupt and condescending manner.

"I am the second chef, and you must be the new skivvy," he said. "Do not speak to me when I am on duty unless I ask you to: just do what you are told and don't get in my way and we will get along."

Well, that threw me back a bit... Charming, I thought to myself; what a brilliant start to my new career in the Merchant Navy! My instincts were right the first time about this fella: this obese five–foot four little shit in the cheap suit from Larne, who had appeared from nowhere, was going to be a right little ray of sunshine. Before I could say anything, he had disappeared as quickly as he had appeared, back to his cabin with his mug of tea. But for all the weight he was carrying, he did impress me with his speed.

Tommy winked at me, grinned and waved his hand as if to say, "don't you worry about him."

It was bitterly cold that evening when we left our Belfast mooring to cross the Irish sea to Heysham harbour in Lancashire. The crossing usually took about eight hours, carrying passengers and various cargoes.

It was a reasonably big galley I was standing in, and was of course the first galley I had ever seen. To my eyes it looked gigantic: it was L– shaped, and the top of the galley was adjacent to the top of the ship's pantry which was also shaped like an L. The bottom of the galley ended in a cul–de–sac and that was where I was stationed with my big sinks in which to wash my dirty dishes and recipients.

We started getting busy quite quickly; Tommy had all sorts of pots and pans on the hob and food in the oven. Old George was putting dishes containing food and plates containing food on the heated table beside the hob, and from there the stewards would collect it to serve to the passengers in the first–class restaurant. Before long I was deep into pots and all sorts of cooking utensils. I was discovering that this was pretty hard work; those pots were not light. I was, but they were not: I was a slip of a lad and everything was big to me back then.

The crew were big, the ship was big, the Irish Sea was big and terribly rough most of the time. Before I knew it, thankfully, the shift was over. Passengers had been fed. Tommy, Old George and I had a sandwich, washed down with a welcoming mug of tea. Tommy handed me a mop and bucket and told me to give the floor a quick rub.

"It's not too dirty or sticky, so just go over it quickly, Ken, and after that go and get your head down."

So that was my first night at sea. I stored the mop and bucket away and proceeded to my cabin. I was ready for a sleep: that had been the most strenuous work I had ever done. I was exhausted.

When I entered the cabin Tommy was already snoring, so I quickly changed into my pyjamas, and climbed quietly up the bunk ladder to my top bunk, praying that I would not fall out. Although I had never slept on a ship before, my fatigue and the motion of the ship soon lulled me to Neverland.

I was soon to discover as the days passed that Tommy never spent much time in our cabin. Most nights after leaving Belfast and when the shift was over, Tommy would be cuddling up with a pretty young stewardess called Agnes in her quarters.

That was just fine with me and of course just fine with Agnes.

Chapter Four

England

THE NEXT MORNING, after a surprisingly restful night's sleep, I was awakened by Tommy's alarm clock, and was relieved to find myself still in my bunk and not on the floor. This was a first of two kinds for me: sleeping up in the air, and not having to share a bed.

Breakfast was prepared for those passengers who had time to spare before they caught a train, coach or were met by car. The crew had to be fed, of course, and Old George would sometimes consent to cook a few sausages, bacon and eggs. I would give the old boy a hand with this and wash up as we went along. But it is a wonder that we ever got anything done, for every few minutes Old George would ask me to fill his mug with tea. Old George loved his tea and drank more of it than a human being should safely consume, and he drank out of a mug that was definitely a health hazard. The mug had, I would guess, started out as a bright, shiny white implement; now it was completely black and riddled with chips. However, Old George was an absolute joy for this young lad to work with. He did not boss me around, he did not belittle me; he was laughing most of the time, telling me risqué jokes, minding his

20

own business, and not giving a damn about anything: a fine way to be, whether young or old...

The pantry department, which I will mention later, was adjacent to the galley, and crew members who did not want a cooked breakfast could have cereals which they would take to their own canteen to eat, although they could have saved themselves a journey because they had cereals and tea making facilities in the canteen.

As time went by, this was the pattern that was set and I adapted to it quite naturally. Nobody really bothered me as long as I was doing my work. The ship docked at Heysham harbour at about seven or eight in the morning. After the passengers had disembarked the rest of the day belonged to the crew.

I walked down the gangplank, put my feet on English soil for the first time in my life and proceeded back up the gangplank and onto the ship. I did not kiss the ground as the Pope does when he arrives in a country; I thought that would be taking things a bit too far.

I carried out this gesture to say that I had actually been ashore in England, albeit for a few seconds (little did I know that one day I would settle in England for more than half my life and bring up a family there.) I was a country boy born in a little village called Crumlin in Northern Ireland and this was a big thing for me. I was like the first man on the moon, however brief the landing might have been. I could not have imagined that soon I would see much stranger, exotic moons. But for now never mind Japan, America, the Panama Canal and all the other countries that I would sail to one day; at the time England was abroad to me.

After that historic expedition, I stayed on board for the first few weeks until I found my feet and then I would venture into Heysham village, and then later into Morecambe, the seaside resort just a few short miles away.

That evening the ship left Heysham for Belfast, once again an overnight crossing, and arrived in Belfast more or less the same time that it had arrived in Heysham the day before. Everything on board ship was well regulated and organised, and I began to feel a routine and to enjoy my days and nights on board.

21

When the ship docked at Heysham, Tommy Burke would be getting ready to go home for the day. Joe Burns would start preparing lunch for the crew who stayed on board. Tommy would hop on an early train for Liverpool to spend the day with his wife. He would join the ship again in the evening. When the ship docked in Belfast, Joe Burns would be getting ready to catch a bus or train to Larne. Exactly the same procedure again, but in reverse. Tommy Burke would start preparing lunch for the crew who stayed on board. When the ship arrived in Belfast, Joe Burns really did not hang about: he was off that vessel quicker than a rat up a drainpipe.

Old George, on the other hand, did not go anywhere. He lived on the ship. No relatives to speak of, none to whom he was close at least. The ship was the old boy's home, and he rarely stepped ashore: he never felt the need to.

When Tommy was cooking, I was learning. Tommy did encourage me in between washing the pots and keeping the galley tidy. Watch and learn, he would say, watch and learn, Kenny. Tommy would actually take the time to demonstrate, when he had the time, and tell me to ask questions if I was not sure about something. From time to time he let me have a turn on the hob. I enjoyed this tremendously and through this method picked things up very quickly.

Joe Burns, on the other hand, was the exact opposite from Tommy: there was no way this man was going to teach me anything at all about cooking. He would not under any circumstances let me near the ovens. This was his territory. He restricted me to the washing up: my station, as he would say. So when Tommy Burke was preparing food, I was learning and enjoying the experience. When Burns was cooking, I was, unless he wanted me to clean the stove or tidy the galley, banished from his domain.

Old George, like Tommy, encouraged me too. When Tommy and Old George were cooking, I could walk about the galley freely provided I kept up with my duties. Old George never stopped surprising me, and he helped the other cooks when it suited him.

The sight of Old George coming into the galley was indeed a sight to behold. When I had first met him he was dressed like a tramp: dirty trousers, dirty house slippers and a filthy cardigan that was full of holes. But what I could never imagine, and what really threw me, was that the old boy would be wearing this gear when he was cooking in the galley: a cook on a passenger ship dressed like a hobo. The Purser or anyone else would never take Old George to task because of his attire. They would have had his friend Tommy Burke to deal with and that wouldn't have been wise or good for their health.

Clothes do not make the man, and every time I saw Old George he put a smile on my face. He told me jokes which made me laugh. But it was his appearance that had me doubled up with laughter at times.

Old George was a genuine street urchin, albeit the oldest one in the world by about sixty–five years; but nevertheless he was the genuine article. A world away from Burns, who was hard work and best avoided. He was sullen, arrogant and remote. He seldom spoke to me, and when he did he spoke quite quickly and in a hurry to get his words out.

Most of the time I could not understand a word he was saying and it was hard work trying to translate, so I was glad we would never be friends: it would have exhausted me. Burns, it seemed to me, did not like youth, although the truth is that he did not get on with most people. I was extremely glad Tommy and Old George were on board that ship.

When you are young you are immortal. When you are old you are not.

Old George was old, but he was also young.

Chapter Five

The Pantry Man

I WAS ENJOYING myself on board ship, going back and forth across the Irish Sea. When the passengers had been fed and everyone had more or less sorted where they would settle themselves for the night, I would take a stroll along the decks and have a chat with the odd passenger and hear their life stories before I turned in for the night.

The Irish Sea, when it has a mind to, can be one of the roughest seas in the world, and although I should not say it, I often derived perverse pleasure from watching a passenger hanging over the ship's side and discharging the meal they had just eaten. And quite a few passengers on a rough night could be sick.

I was getting to know a few of the crew. Most of them were civil to me and, despite my youth and inexperience, conversed with me in an adult fashion; this of course filled me with confidence. But as always you will encounter one or two obnoxious individuals in any workplace, and a ship is no exception. I had already met Joe Burns. The two individuals I will mention here were truly odious and unpopular, as I was about to learn. They were called Mick Mullan and John Kerr. Mick Mullan was a fireman employed in the engine room; a fireman and a donkey man who assisted the ship's engineers. John Kerr was the guy in charge of the ship's pantry department; for some unknown reason, he liked to be referred to as 'the pantry man'.

John Kerr had a couple of lads employed in the pantry department; they were both nineteen years old. John Kerr's department joined with the galley and would serve salads, sandwiches, pots of tea and coffee, cakes, etc. The stewards would come into the pantry and galley and collect the food to serve to the passengers in the first class restaurant, which was conveniently situated just through a pantry door

The pantry man did not treat his two staff with any degree of respect. He would panic even when things were running smoothly at the beginning of a shift. When things really started getting busy (which was the case almost every night), he would start shouting, cursing and even pushing anyone who was in his line of fire. Invariably most of the time it was the two lads, Tom and Jack, who took the flack, but the stewards and anyone else who happened to be in the vicinity also came under fire. He really should not have been on board a ship, and although he was in his late forties, I suspected that this was his first ship. How he got away with this behaviour, day after day, week after week, baffled me.

He was a huge man and he could really roar when he lost it, and this was what intimidated most people. However, this situation would change in the most unexpected way one evening.

At the start of the shift, Tom and Jack and I were deep in conversation as we often were, but on this occasion I had wandered right into the pantry. We were having a laugh when Kerr bounced over and just missed my face with his hand, and shouted at me to "fuck off back into the fucking galley," which I promptly did. He had finally flipped, I thought to myself.

Unknown to Kerr, Tommy Burke had witnessed this affray, and made a dash for him. Fortunately for Kerr, he was faster than the speed of light, which was impressive for a big man, and he was able to escape and disappear from sight. Tommy did not even bother to pursue, knowing the Pantry Man would have to appear sometime. This was the first time I had seen Tommy go for someone, and that someone was Kerr who frightened most people most of the time. I would soon discover that no one ever messed with Tommy Burke, and fortunately for me, Tommy Burke was going to be my guardian and bodyguard.

About half an hour later John Kerr did come back into the pantry with the Chief Purser. Of course John Kerr was stood wisely and closely behind the Chief Purser, shaking with fear. The Chief Purser walked over to Tommy and asked him would he accept an apology; Tommy smirked and reluctantly said that he would. The Chief Purser then dragged a petrified Kerr over and demanded he apologise to Tommy and the boy, yours truly. This he did with shaking hands and wobbly knees.

After this incident it started to dawn on me that Tommy Burke was someone who would take no nonsense from anyone, and I believed that he was prepared to do this with his fists. The talking might come later. As for me, I was certainly relieved that I worked with Tommy, who I knew from that moment on would make sure I came to no harm. This was indeed so. The Pantry Man never bothered me again, and from time to time Tommy would give him that glare, just enough to let him know that he would always be on his case. In fact, on occasions John Kerr tried, in his fumbling way, to be civil to me. This was something that he did not practice with the two unfortunate lads who worked with him.

Over time his demeanour did improve, for a diplomatic visit from Tommy was something the Pantry Man would not wish to be repeated.

Chapter Six

Bungalow

TOM AND JACK and I became good friends. We were probably the youngest members of the crew, and I was certainly the youngest. They both came from Belfast, so we had something in common. We would have long conversations about the districts we came from and what it was like in our schooldays. Tom had been brought up in the Falls Road district, and Jack hailed from the Shankill Road area. Any topic remotely religious or anything relating to religion was never discussed or debated. I believe that being away from Ireland changed our attitudes and broadened our minds.

When our duties were finished in the morning, and when we had the afternoon off, we would nip into Heysham village. There was a café there which served nettle wine and we loved that particular drop of pop. This was the first time that I had drunk wine, albeit one of a stingy, nettle variety. The French Bordeaux, Cabernet Sauvignon and Claret would come much later.

When we had an odd night off we would travel into Morecambe. Jack was nineteen and already on the whiskey chasers. A pint of the black stuff and a whiskey and Jack was in heaven. He introduced Tom and me to this seductive and deadly combination and we did enjoy it.

I was probably sixteen years old, yet nobody in any public house ever asked me for identification to prove that I was the legal age to drink. Our drinking was modest, but Jack could drink from opening to closing time and was never much affected. He was one of those fellas who are good with the drink: he laughed and joked and never got punchy or argumentative. Great company on a night out.

Tom and Jack had happy dispositions, despite having to put up with a boss like John Kerr; but as I have mentioned, after the pantry man's brush with Tommy Burke, this all changed. The Chief Purser warned John Kerr his attitude would improve towards his staff and other crew members immediately, or he would be leaving the ship.

Change it did from that moment. John Kerr became a new personality. From that day onwards he never shouted again, seldom lost his temper; and treated Tom and Jack and other crew members with the respect they deserved.

Tom and Jack had joined the ship about three months before me and had got to know quite a few of the crew. They told me categorically with emphasis to watch out for Mick Mullan, as he was a scary bit of work. In Jack's own words, he was a psychopath. Although he had never spoke before to Mullan, he had passed him one day, and got a stare that nearly stopped him in his tracks.

On the Duke of Rothesay there was a little stairway between the galley and the rear starboard deck. The stairway led to the crew's quarters down below. Outside there was a little bench which I would sit on to have my tea break and enjoy the cool air. I would sit on that bench with a welcome mug of tea in one hand and a cigarette in the other, enjoying the blissful respite from the routine of work.

One morning, I proceeded from the galley, three steps across the stairway and on to the outside deck to sit on my bench. But it was already occupied by a gigantic man whose dimensions left no room for anyone else to share the bench, and this was at least a two–seater. This was Mick Mullan, just as Jack had described him: about five feet ten inches tall, although to me he looked five feet ten inches wide as well.

Never before had I seen such an enormous man as this.

To me he looked like a bungalow. The only difference was this bungalow had a head on top. This bungalow was perched on my bench, which to my knowledge he had never sat on before and from which he immediately shouted at me to piss off, a request to which I speedily responded without further ado.

Tommy was surprised, and remarked how quick my tea break had been, to which I replied that it had been a wee bit too nippy out there. I did not mention Mick Mullan.

Two days later I cautiously ventured out to my bench and was met by the same greeting: piss off, twat! I pissed off quickly. This had been my favourite spot and it had been taken over by a man to whom I had never spoken before.

Back in the galley, Tommy once again asked me what was going on, observing how it had been an even quicker tea break than before.

"Bloody nippy, Tommy," I replied. Only this time it was not nippy: the sun was shining, and anyway Tommy would have figured out that the weather had never bothered me before.

I told myself that this guy was not going to get the better of me, and two days later, mug in one hand, cigarette in the other, I proceed across the stairway to my bench once again. The Neanderthal was spread out on my bench, wiping the sweat from his face with an oily rag which they use in the engine room. This time he stood up, stuck his chest out and once again invited me to vacate the vicinity in colourful terms. But on this occasion, Tommy suddenly appeared and was met with the same greeting.

"Fuck off, scouse!" was Mullan's immediate reply.

The Bungalow bellowed back at Tommy: a big mistake. As soon as the word "scouse" had left Mullan's mouth, Tommy had landed a devastating right–hand punch on Mullan's head which immediately separated The Bungalow's body from his senses: he fell in a heap on the deck.

"I have wanted to do that for a long time, and now was a good a time as any," Tommy quipped nonchalantly as Mullan lay flattened out on the deck, and walked back into the galley.

The Bungalow must have been unconscious for quite a while. About two minutes later I heard something outside. I stuck my head out to have a look but The Bungalow with a head on had gone. I never saw or heard from The Bungalow again, and about a fortnight later he discharged himself from the ship.

Once again my boss had come to my rescue; he was my bodyguard, mentor and teacher.

I could not have had a better start.

Chapter Seven

Chief Rubin

THE PANTRY MAN was subdued considerably after his altercation with Tommy Burke, my boss. His personality had changed miraculously, if that is possible, to pleasant, meek and mannerly. Tom and Jack, his two pantry lads, could not believe the change that had come over their boss and were now really enjoying their daily work.

The Pantry Man, of course, had heard of Mick Mullan's run in with Tommy and must have been thanking his lucky stars that he escaped the punch that Mullan took instead. That blow to The Bungalow's head had resulted in a broken nose and severely swollen jaw, and although The Bungalow was remarkably ugly before the punch landed, this did not improve his looks at all.

Although the Pantry Man had been an arrogant fool, he was also extremely vain, and now, looking at Mullan's face, he was going to make sure he would walk on the side of prudence. Another run–in with Tommy Burke was something to be avoided at all costs, especially as it could have disastrous results for him. A punch or two from Tommy and the Pantry Man's good looks would vanish forever, not to mention his good health.

I have mentioned the Chief Purser a few times so far, but he wasn't a Chief Purser; if you stretched your imagination you could call him, with tongue in cheek, a purser: a ship's officer in charge of accounts. We will take the chief away and call him a purser, but in truth no one seemed to know what his title was. If anything, he was in charge of the catering staff.

The title Chief Purser came about because one day he asked Jack to make him a sandwich and a cup of tea, and Jack said, "Right away, Chief!"

Now Rubin, which was his real name, liked this form of address from Jack, especially as there were other people within earshot, and he beamed quite happily whenever it was used. So it caught on and before long everyone was calling him 'Chief.' It was mischief really, but Rubin was blissfully unaware of this.

The ritual did not last long. Rubin was not a chief of anything: he was a self–appointed boss of everything and everybody. 'Purser' was a mouthful, so eventually it reverted to Rubin, much warmer than 'Purser.' Rubin of course did not like this: going from Chief Purser to Purser and then to Rubin. The brass cheek of it, he would say; peasants, he would murmur under his breath. At least they could call me 'Mister,' he would plead with whoever would listen, but this wasn't going to happen. Rubin it was, like it or lump it, with love.

One day Rubin rushed into the pantry, foaming at the mouth, telling everyone within earshot that our ship would soon be leaving for Scotland and the Scottish Isles. Of course, everyone already knew this, but acted surprised when he told us the news.

Nobody wanted to upset Rubin, because despite his little quirks and eccentricities he was basically a good old boy and well–liked by everyone. Rubin could be infuriating, but he was also endearing. I liked Rubin the Purser; most of the crew liked Rubin the Purser. He would dash all over the place like a man possessed, but that was his way.

I soon realised why Rubin was getting himself worked up. It was because he had never travelled anywhere further than Heysham and Belfast. This Scottish mini–cruise would be about ten days, and Rubin had never been away from his village, Heysham, any longer than two days; in fact, he was a Heysham man through and through and proud of it. One day he boasted to Tom, Jack and I that he rarely opened his pay packet. How daft, I thought to myself.

That was in the good old days when you received your weekly or fortnightly wages wrapped up in a brown envelope. I would open my pay packet as soon as it was handed to me to check its contents, as I suspected everyone else did. It was a sensible practice to ensure that you had not been accidentally, or deliberately, underpaid. If there was a discrepancy, for instance, if any overtime worked had not been paid, or just a simple mistake, then you could query it immediately. If you were overpaid, and if you were not stupid, you would not of course query it. This rarely happened.

Rubin was the only one on board ship that did not check his wages, and I thought that he was a smart cookie! We, of course, asked him in unison why he rarely opened his pay packets. He began to explain to us that he had married a woman a few years older than himself, and the reason for this was that she had some money behind her.

He went on to say, "Why not use her money first?"

Now I was a naïve young lad, but even I could not see the logic in that statement. His wife, apart from being simple, must have been a very understanding and forgiving person.

Shortly after that revelation I began to picture the characters that had so far in a short space of time crossed my path.

There was John Kerr, the Pantry Man: an arrogant, vain, shouting fool, who because of his lucky escape from Tommy Burke and threatened with the sack by Rubin, had turned over a new leaf, and slowly but surely his attitude towards his staff had changed for the better.

Then there was Mick Mullan, The Bungalow with a head on who had a violent personality and became apoplectic with rage at the slightest provocation. He left the ship two weeks after being on the wrong end of a right hand from Tommy Burke.

And there was Rubin who, to we, his colleagues, appeared on the outside to be a very nice man, although I had learnt about his not opening pay packets, saving his own earnings and letting his wife pay for everything. This was pure greed and selfishness. Even to this young lad, his behaviour did not seem right or appropriate. After his revelation, my opinion of him changed somewhat. I still liked him, but wondered what life was like for him and his wife when he arrived home every other day.

Even in the short time I had been on the ship, I thought to myself, these three adults had started to change my perspective about some of the creatures who inhabit our planet. In three human beings I had encountered arrogance, vanity, bullying, violence, selfishness and, last but not least, greed. Sometimes people are not what they appear to be; often, in fact.

In two thousand years, human behaviour has not changed that much: today we just wear different clothes.

Chapter Eight

Scotland Ahoy

THE DUKE OF Rothesay was built at William Denny and Brothers Dumbarton and completed in 1956. She was designed to operate as both a passenger ferry (primarily on the Heysham – Belfast route) and as a cruise ship. She operated from 1956 to 1979. Her sister ships were The Duke of Argyll and The Duke of Lancaster. They were also on the Heysham – Belfast route and of course they also cruised to Europe.

The gross tonnage of The Duke of Rothesay was 4,797 tons. She could carry approximately fifteen hundred passengers, which for her size was extraordinary; they were well squeezed in. This is especially significant when you see cruise ships of today. Quite a few of them are well over one hundred thousand tonnes: they are floating towns, ten times the weight of my ship but only carry up to one thousand passengers. The Duke of Rothesay and her sister ships The Duke of Argyll and The Duke of Lancaster were stars in their time, and the last steamers catering solely for passengers built for British Railways (at that time also a ferry operator.)

In her capacity as a cruise ship she would be touring the

Scottish Isles and further afield in continental Europe. Scottish cruises were about ten days in duration and European cruises about fourteen days.

When the Dukes were required for cruising, many cabins were transformed into bathrooms for adjacent cabins. Big changes were achieved in only a few days. With the flick of a switch you could control the temperature in your cabin. The first–class dining room and the cafeteria–combined lounge were superbly designed and were of faultless taste. There were tea, coffee and food dispensers for those passengers who preferred something lighter than a set meal. The ship had stabilising fins, which helped to reduce the turbulence in very rough seas. These stabilisers were very useful and very welcome when the ship was thrashing back and forth across the Irish Sea to Belfast or Heysham with fifteen hundred passengers, as she did in her heyday.

So soon we would be off to Scotland and the Isles. Rubin was excited, everyone was excited; that is, all of us whose furthest destinations visited to date were Heysham and Belfast. And Scotland proved to be beautiful: we sailed to Glasgow, Greenock, Oban and Fort William. 'The Fort', whose town lies at the foot of Ben Nevis, is a beautiful location, as is Oban. Cruising through the Scottish Isles at the start of spring was a grand experience; the weather was pleasant with plenty of sunshine.

At that time of year in Scotland it could very well have been snowing, but it was not. I recall that the landscape was as lush and green as Ireland. Well, almost! I went ashore in all these ports albeit for a brief period, according to my ships' duties, although Oban and Fort William did leave an enduring memory. These two locations would make an impression on anyone in any part of the world.

Everything went well on board ship, although it was slightly strange at first to see the same passengers out and about, day and night. The food was good: of course there was Tommy Burke, a good chef, and Old George, who despite his unkempt appearance could cook when required. They were joined by two company chefs. Old George was kept on the fringe and he concentrated most of the time on keeping the crew well fed and happy. I helped him when I was not washing or mopping and when I had a minute or two, I would be watching the other chefs going about their work.

Another good thing about this trip from my perspective was the absence of Joe Burns: apparently he was on sick leave. Rubin was in his element, over the moon with his brand spanking new uniform, walking along the deck and conversing with passengers, registering any complaints they might have had, although luckily for all of us the complaints were few and far between.

I always thought Rubin would welcome the odd passenger complaint. Perhaps a cabin carpet might not have been vacuumed or their bacon was cold. Then he would hastily go to whichever department or individual the complaint was registered against and give them a good bollocking, in his own sweet, inimitable way and knowing that he would not be told impolitely to vacate the premises in return. Because, as he told everyone time and time again, this was not Belfast to Heysham: this is the big time, we are cruising now. These passengers, he continually told everyone (and remember, it was hard to find the gaps when this man was not preaching), are paying good money, and have to be treated with courtesy, good manners and respect.

Rubin had found his niche; he was in his own, self–satisfied element, and at such times I did honestly think that Chief Rubin thought he was the captain of the ship. But soon we would be back on the Heysham – Belfast route for a month or two, before the vessel was transformed once more into a cruise ship for her European cruise, and then Rubin would be brought back to reality.

On the Scottish cruise Rubin had been billed, through his insistence and that of the captain, as "Chief Steward." Now everyone wondered what he was going to be like on the European cruise. Until that time came, he would be called Rubin, or at least to his face…

Chapter Nine

The Last Time I Saw Billy

CRUISING AROUND THE Scottish isles was a wonderful experience for the country boy from Crumlin; they are a beautiful part of the British Isles. We were heading back to England for a spot of refitting and then on to Belfast when I decided that I needed a break.

A ten day Scottish cruise is not a three months cruise, but it was a completely new world to me, and constant hard work. Besides, I had been in the Merchant Navy several months now without a rest, so I decided that I needed a short holiday to catch up with old mates. I had been away from my mother for ten days, twelve days altogether, and I missed her. Goodness me, I was homesick: a real mummy's boy. So I got myself three days leave. Tommy Burke didn't mind: he and Old George could cover my absence.

I had only been away a short time, but approaching Belfast, her harbours and the sight of the giant cranes of Harland and Wolff, greatly pleased my eyes.

I got home in the morning. My Da was at work. I got a "hello Kenny" from my mother. Everyone else was already out or at work. My mother told me that Billy McCann had called at our home almost every day to enquire if I was going out. My mother, brothers and sisters had told him every day when he called for me that I was at sea. Now anyone else would have stopped calling after being told the first time, but not Billy: his head was in the clouds.

The red wine which he was beginning to enjoy was probably interfering with his logic. A few months ago, just before I had first joined my ship, Billy had been buying cheap plonk and devouring it with relish. Of course he would offer me some, but a mouthful immediately told my taste buds that it was not for me, not this particular liquid. I would be enjoying my first drink soon enough, but not this beverage that Billy adored.

Billy had had a hard life, and I say that without flippancy. We all struggled in those years, but Billy had been at war with his siblings all through his childhood.

The chance to escape came via the Lyceum Picture House, thanks to his sister Kathleen, who was of course his favourite girl. Kathleen was able to obtain a constant supply of free cinema tickets for her brother because of her close relationship with the cinema manager.

Billy spent as many hours as he could in the cinema. Here he was safe from the menacing school bullies on the rare occasion when he did turn up for school, and the constant arguing and fighting at home. Billy also had a hard time trying to avoid the school inspector who was knocking at his door every week. There in the cinema he could relax, forget about everything, and dream, with the odd Woodbine cigarette stuck in his mouth.

It was ironic that when I was away Billy would call for me, and when I was at home, which at the beginning was every other day (except of course for the ten–day Scottish cruise and the twelve–day European cruise), Billy never called for me.

Strange, Billy.

So on the first day of my three day break, it was I who called on Billy. He opened the door and broke into a broad grin. We were old friends and mighty glad to see each other after such a long time.

"Hello Kenny, bloody glad to see you! Where have you

been? I have been calling for you for months and they keep telling me you're away. Away where to, Kenny?"

So once more I informed Billy that I was in the Merchant Navy and that I was home every other day, but we kept missing each other. It sort of sank in, but then I thought it had sunk in before. I was worried for my old mate, my best mate: he just did not seem to comprehend my explanation.

Billy and I went for a long walk and talked about old times. We both recalled our little newspaper racket, where we went all over Belfast collecting old newspapers and magazines to sell for recycling. We talked about Annie Hughes – oh, how we loved to talk about Annie... Billy said she was still bloody lovely. I said that I had not seen her for a long time and would try to see her in the next day or two. Then I asked Billy how his sister Kathleen was getting on. She had gone to England. But to everyone's surprise, not least that of her family, she had returned home to Belfast.

"As you know, Kenny," Billy told me, "she went to England with her mate to escape our feuding family and start afresh and end her relationship with the cinema manager. He being a stupid chump, he pursued her to England, and after a few weeks had managed to come back to Belfast and take up her old position at the cinema, which he had held open. He really was stricken with my sister."

I nodded, fascinated by the ongoing annals of the family saga.

"I tell you what, Kenny, when he was away on extended leave chasing my sister in England, I was left chewing my fingers to the bone, because my supply of free complimentary cinema tickets had expired. So my daft sister Kathleen had been in England only about a month when her even dafter old boyfriend, the cinema manager, decided he couldn't live without her. So what with her being away a month and him taking two weeks to persuade her to come back home to Belfast, I was without cinema tickets for about six weeks." I nodded once more in sympathy with Billy's plight. "I'll tell you Kenny, I didn't forgive them for a while, but that was short lived, as Kathleen was reinstated in her job at the picture house and my supply of cinema tickets began to roll in again."

"Where do you get your supply of wine from?" I asked Billy. Billy was too young to buy it over the counter. He informed that an old dipso would get into Lynch's pub every night, and would sell him a bottle whenever he wanted.

"It's cheap!" Billy explained. "I befriended the old bugger. He was so drunk one night, he could hardly stand, and not one person volunteered to help him, so I escorted him home, carried him over my shoulder almost the whole way to his house. He only lived about half a mile from the pub. He remembered this kindness, supplied me with wine, and cheaply, whenever I required it."

I could not believe these words were coming from my old friend's mouth.

"I saw your face squirm when I first offered you a drink from the bottle," Billy said. "It's hard to take at first. It's an acquired taste, and anyway I can't get through most days without it…"

Billy was seventeen years old, give or take a month or two, and he was telling me that he could not exist without a bottle of wine. I felt dreadful for my dear friend Billy, a simple soul who had never really spoken badly of or hurt anyone. I know one's fate is one's own responsibility, but I think fate was taking Billy somewhere he could not resist going…

Over the next few weeks I did see Billy; from time to time I made a point of doing that. We visited the cinema again, courtesy of Kathleen, of course. Billy's face was visibly red and slightly bloated, and his hands were shaking. The drink was telling. The continental cruise would be starting soon. I would be away for a couple of weeks. But that was the last time I was to see Billy.

Billy succumbed to the drink: three years later, while I was abroad, Billy fell ill and died. Alcohol can be enjoyed when taken in sensible amounts, but is terribly cruel to the weak amongst us. For some people life can be a constant bugger; for most of us it can be a bugger from time to time.

For my friend Billy, life was not good: save for some free cinema tickets, it was a remorseless shit.

Chapter Ten

The Cruise

I **SAID GOODBYE** to Billy. I did not get a chance to see anyone else as I was with him during most of my three–day break. I never even caught a glimpse of Annie Hughes. That was a disappointment, but I promised myself that I would make the effort to call into her shop to see her whenever I next had the opportunity.

The cruise was about to get under way, but before that we would make our way to Holyhead on the Isle of Anglesey where the ship was to go into dry dock for a fortnight. I suppose this was her first inspection, a routine scrape of the barnacles, or minor cosmetic and engineering updates. With these refurbishments, we spent a fortnight in Holyhead: a pleasant little town, very quiet with nothing much going on; a visit to the pubs, a walk around town. My friends and I stayed aboard ship for most of the fortnight.

We were now ready to start our cruise. We picked up a new member of the crew in Holyhead, a steward named Tommy Bryce, and then headed for Heysham. One of our stewards had gone on sick leave while we were tied up in Holyhead: hence the reason for Tommy Bryce joining the ship in Wales. He was comparatively young, but very well turned out; he took his duties seriously and carried them out with gusto. He was of slim build but appeared to have a beer belly.

Rubin was flapping around all over the ship, annoying everyone, even before we reached Heysham, where all of the cruise passengers would be embarking. Of course, he made it clear once again to everyone on board via a memo that he was not be addressed as Rubin. "Chief Steward" was his title once again, by order of the captain.

And Rubin? You could say that Rubin, although not a bad or nasty person in any sense of the word, was slightly narcissistic. He was the centre of his own universe; that may sound extreme, but he did use people to a certain extent.

When we docked in Heysham in the early morning everything was shipshape and ready to go. Passengers would start boarding that afternoon. But Rubin was a man possessed; he had gone from a reasonable man to a gibbering wreck, and the passengers had not even arrived yet. With his smart new Chief Steward's uniform and his shiny shoes he looked even smarter than the captain; perhaps that was his intention all along. I had a feeling, as did the rest of the catering staff, that if Rubin did not relax a little, he would be heading for a breakdown or a cardiac arrest.

At approximately noon that day the first passengers started boarding: well–heeled and well–dressed, their jewellery flashing everywhere. No coaches or buses arriving at these docks: only private cars and taxis.

In the days when I was young most people could not afford to take a taxi, let alone buy a car, and walking or perhaps a bus was the transport of the poor. Ordinary working–class people and the middle classes could only dream of going on a cruise, and it is only recently that the cruise experience has moved to within reach of the middle classes.

Well, they were coming on board now, those women dressed in their real fur coats and their fox furs draped around their shoulders. That is a spectacle you rarely see now if at all: women wearing dead animals on their bodies. What a sight for a ragamuffin from Belfast: all these rich people parading around. I could not resist a peek from the galley at the expensive clothes, furs and glittering jewellery. A sight for sore eyes. A sight for poor eyes.

Rubin was to look after the passengers when the ship set sail, to see they were settled and that his staff were performing. But Rubin just could not resist standing near the gangplank and watching all this money coming aboard. I watched them, and I watched him watching them, with fascination.

At around about three o'clock we were on our way, heading for Rouen, Amsterdam, Rotterdam, Antwerp and Esbjerg, before the final port of call, Ostend. Rubin was having a great time while the rest of his staff was working all hours. Thankfully because of his creeping we rarely saw Rubin. He was behaving as if he was a passenger. I watched him ingratiate himself on several occasions with passengers, and found it all very embarrassing. He seemed to be in their company twenty four hours a day.

Meanwhile, when I was not observing Rubin, Tommy Burke and his chefs seemed to be in the galley day and night, and I was cooking for the crew with occasional help from Old George.

The reason I was cooking now, albeit for the crew and not the passengers, was because Tommy told me that I would be promoted to assistant cook when we arrived back in Heysham after the cruise. This cheered me up no end, so cooking for the crew, provided I did not poison them, was a task I did not mind, and I tackled it with enthusiasm and zeal.

The crew were quite content with simple well cooked food. To start them off for the day I cooked them a sturdy Irish breakfast. Lunches would be stews, lasagne, cottage and shepherd pies, and on occasion a good old sausage and mash.

Tommy Burke and his staff did put in some hours, but they did not have the handicap of Rubin interfering and giving orders: Rubin was sensible enough not to annoy Tommy under any circumstances, as the Chief Steward in the very least knew that he would have been told unceremoniously to leave, and, worse–case scenario if he persisted, his face would have been introduced to one of Tommy's right handers. Fortunately for those slaving within its hothouse conditions, the galley was at least one area on the ship which was a no–go area for Rubin, although when he behaved himself, and this he did in the company of Tommy, he was treated well by the galley head honcho.

Tommy Burke could not under any mitigating circumstances tolerate fools, irrespective of what their position was on board ship and with the possible exception of the officers and captain, and then only if he was having a good day.

We had a great time visiting these countries. Tom and Jack and I went ashore in all these locations if only for two or three hours most of the time. But what a wonderful thrill for three young lads from Belfast.

This European cruise left a lasting impression on the young me. I enjoyed every destination and still recall them to this day.

Amsterdam, with its numerous narrow streets and the canals that cross them was really beautiful. Rotterdam, illuminated at night, turned out to be a wonderful sight. Rouen, pretty, quiet and idyllic, sitting on the river Seine, and Antwerp, with the Cathedral of our Lady. We only had about an hour in Esbjerg but it seemed a pleasant seaport town. The port of Ostend in Belgium was to be the last destination on our European cruise and what a lovely little town it was to end the trip.

The captain had decided that because of everything having gone so well and the fact that we were ahead of schedule, the ship would lie in Ostend for two days and nights. This would give the passengers plenty of time to see the sights, go shopping, and perhaps take a trip to Bruges. It also meant that most of the crew would at least see some of the town: you need a happy crew to run a ship well. It had been a successful cruise with no complaints, which was unusual for a first cruise. The passengers had been well fed, watered and looked after; Rubin and his staff had seen to that, and he had been congratulated by the captain.

For Rubin, that was as good as being knighted by the Queen. However, all the catering staff of which Rubin was the boss, and I dare say most of the crew, had seen a new side to the Chief Steward, and we all concluded that Chief Steward Rubin was a big snob from little Heysham.

We arrived in Ostend around noon. Most of the passengers had lunch and then disembarked. Old George and I arranged with the crew that we would give them a cold tea: a salad, cold meats, etc. We would lay it out on their dining table and they could help themselves as they came off duty. This seemed to satisfy all of them, and this arrangement enabled Old George and I to finish early, shower, shave and head into town. Well, I would be heading for town; Old George would be heading for his cabin to keep a bottle of whiskey for company.

As I left the ship for town I could see the attractive sight of the two towers of the town's main church, the Church of Saint Peter and Saint Paul. These two towers nestled quite comfortably in the town of Ostend, where we hoped to find rest and recreation, but would instead experience the illogical unpleasantness of simply rotten human behaviour.

Chapter Eleven

Bad Guy

W E HAD ARRIVED in Ostend in good spirits: it was a successful cruise, the passengers were happy and the crew had performed their duties well. But that was not to last, at least not for three of the crew: Tom, Jack and I witnessed an incident that evening which would leave us very unhappy and angry.

My two friends and I wandered into the town and entered the first bar we saw; it was really a café–bar: a small, old pub full of atmosphere. There was a small, heavily–built man behind the bar, whom we learnt was the owner. He had a big grin on his face which put us at ease immediately.

We ordered three beers and the landlord told us to sit down at one of the three tables and his daughter would serve us the drinks. A young, rather pretty girl delivered our drinks with a lovely smile, and we could not have been in better spirits: we were halfway through our drinks, enjoying our time ashore and having a welcome break from the routine of our duties on board ship. This was a warm welcome in a new port.

The bar door opened and in strolled three deckhands from

our ship. We were friendly with two of them: they were called Jim and Jim (yes, both of them were called Jim). The other deckhand was called Phil Lavery. We were not friendly with him; no one was friendly with him: he just was not liked on board ship. He was arrogant and known to be a bully. Jim and Jim were good lads and friendly blokes and we were surprised when they walked into the pub with the likes of Lavery.

Jim and Jim went to the bar to order drinks and Lavery stumbled to the toilet. While he was otherwise engaged I asked Jim and Jim what was going on and why they were with him.

"Ken, we didn't have much choice," one of the Jims explained. "We bumped into him in town and despite various efforts we haven't managed to get rid of the idiot."

They ordered their drinks and sat at the table next to ours. The pretty girl brought their drinks to their table and then walked over to the juke box. She put a coin in and selected a ballad.

Lavery approached her and asked her for a dance; his speech was slurred and he was on his way to being very drunk, but the pretty young thing agreed to dance with him out of courtesy. Straightaway his hands were all over the girl; he was slobbering and saliva was running down his chin. I looked at this idiot and then looked at her dad who was also looking at the scene and beginning to get very agitated. There was a severe grimace on his face.

Within just a minute or two of appearing, Lavery had overstepped the mark of decency, and turned a pleasant atmosphere into one of unease and menace.

When the music ended, Lavery invited the girl to join him at their table. Again, and out of courtesy, the girl, looking edgily at her father, accepted the invitation. Lavery held the chair for the girl to sit down and, as she was doing so, Lavery pulled the chair away from her, causing the girl to crash to the floor. Her spine caught the edge of the seat as she fell and she let out an excruciating yell of agony.

Her outraged father leapt over the bar in a flash with a baseball bat in his hand, heading straight for Lavery, who was cringing against the exit door. Jim and Jim, who were tall, well–built lads, managed to subdue the landlord who was fuming with rage. They told us later that the reason they had stopped the landlord from whacking Lavery was not to protect the drunk, but to stop the landlord from getting into trouble if the police arrived. The lads were sure, as was I, that there would have been a murder charge if the landlord had not been subdued.

Jim and Jim sat the girl's father down and apologised profusely for Lavery's behaviour. The landlord's daughter was clearly shocked, but got back on her feet and seemed to be none the worse for wear. I was amazed she had not sustained serious injury to her back. Her fall, even so many years later, seems painfully vivid in my memory.

We left soon afterwards, a bad taste lingering in our mouths. Lavery ran to catch up with us; we still could not get rid of that fool. Jim and Jim told him to piss off quickly before they felt the urge to finish what the young girl's father had almost started. They told me afterwards that they had both came to the same conclusion: they were sorry that they had interfered that night and should have let the father of the young girl do what he was going to do to Lavery.

We never spoke to Lavery again. He turned out to be what we had always suspected: a drunken, cowardly bully. Someone who would pick on and trick a defenceless girl but shy away from a fair fight and a hiding he thoroughly deserved.

For a long time afterwards I thought about the incident in that old bar in Ostend. Jim and Jim told me that they were going to report the incident to the First Officer. I suppose they wanted my reaction. I told them that Tom, Jack and I were alright with that as it was the right thing to do. We were not telling tales out of school or ratting on a shipmate. Lavery was on our ship, but he was no mate. Jim and Jim saw the First Officer who in turn had Lavery report to the bridge to explain his actions. He could not wriggle out of this one. The First Officer told him that his was despicable behaviour which gave us a bad name, and could not and would not be tolerated. Lavery was promptly discharged and escorted off the ship.

The First Officer paid a visit to the bar the next day with a barrage of gifts for the young girl, told her and her father that

49

Lavery had been dealt with most severely, and again apologised. This was a good exercise in public relations: Britain did not need yet another episode of behaving badly abroad.

After all that drama, we would be heading back to Heysham and a few more months of traipsing back and forth over the Irish Sea.

Chapter Twelve

Tommy Twice

TOMMY BRYCE WAS soon named Tommy Twice. Nicknames were invented and commonly used on board ship, and Tommy would be no exception. He had joined our ship when she was in dry dock in Holyhead and being readied for her European cruise.

Tommy had worked in a couple of hotels as a waiter, came with good references and would soon become a favourite of Rubin "the Chief" Steward simply because he was an exceptionally good waiter. Waiter, on land; steward, at sea.

Tommy was perfect for the job: a smile seldom left his face even when he was serving an ill–mannered or tetchy passenger. Although it was a genuine smile, it was also a façade, a pretence, because Tommy's thoughts were always somewhere else far away. Tommy told me day in and day out and anyone else who would listen, and they were few and far between, that his dream was to be a film star. But let us stray from Hollywood for a while and I will tell you why he was nicknamed Tommy Twice.

Tommy repeated everything he would say to you and most of the time everything you would say to him. He did not extend this debilitating habit to the passengers; oh no, it was just the crew that he tortured, and in particular it was the catering staff, with whom Tommy worked every day, who were mostly affected.

For instance, Tommy would greet me with a "Good morning, Ken" and then straightaway follow this up with another "Good morning, Ken. How's it going, Ken?"

"How are things with you, Tommy?" I would enquire, affably enough. "Are you enjoying yourself and getting on well with your job?"

"I'm doing fine, Ken; I'm doing fine."

Eventually, as time went by, I tried to avoid Tommy but it was difficult to hide on board ship. I liked Tommy as did most of his fellow workers; you could not help but like him as he was a kind and pleasant fellow. I only tried to avoid him because he was a serial repeater.

But it was his fellow stewards who worked closely with Tommy who were mostly affected by his polly–parrot mannerisms. Perhaps I was imagining or seeing things, but when his fellow workers came off duty they seemed to be in a mesmerised state, dazed by one repetition after another. Tommy was such an amiable and lovely fellow that his fellow workers simply put up with his strange behaviour.

And Tommy was a dreamer. He wanted to be a film star, to be a famous actor. Not a jobbing actor, not a character actor, but the fella up there on the big screen. Top billing: the film star.

"Ken," he would say, "Ken, I don't want to be waiting on tables all my life. I would like one day to be waited on, waited on, Ken. If and when I become famous I will have a servant or two, servant or two…"

Tommy was deadly serious and had told me that since he was about ten years old, and his mother had started bringing him and his siblings to picture house matinees to see films (mostly about cowboys), he was hooked as soon as the curtains opened. When Tommy talked to me about his dream of being famous, which he did with every opportunity he got, he was not daydreaming but deadly serious and spelt it out to me with conviction.

Tommy had never acted in his life, not even in a school

play, but this was no deterrent to him. He was without doubt a very handsome young man; the important consideration for Tommy was that he knew he was good looking and said that that was the only qualification that was required. Acting skills would come later perhaps, but good looks were the main incentive.

He was probably right, I thought to myself. Many film stars in those days could not be called good or even competent actors; much of their success was due to their physical appearance. The fans went for looks; the girls liked tall, handsome men.

Against my better judgement, I told Tommy that he would have to break the habit of a lifetime, a very unsociable habit, and stop repeating words that he spoke to people and people spoke to him, otherwise his dreams of becoming famous wouldn't become true, or at least not for the reasons he wanted.

Tommy took this advice on board, reacted well to it, and told me from that moment on that he would make every effort to correct this abnormality. Despite this reassurance, I never thought for one moment that Tommy would become a film star, although I went along with it and never told him any differently. Was I to ruin his dream, the thing that made his everyday life more bearable?

Sadly, I was right, and to the best of my knowledge Tommy never did become famous. It was not for the want of trying, especially on his mother's side. She sent photographs and letters relating to her son and any little titbit of information she could think of to film studios here in Britain and especially America.

It was an expensive hobby and in the end all in vain. Did these items ever reach the studios? Were they ever looked at by film directors or producers? I think not. They were probably binned along with thousands of other photographs of hopefuls and dreamers.

Billy McCann, my old childhood mate, had done his dreaming in the Lyceum Picture House on the New Lodge Road. The difference between Tommy and Billy was an ocean wide. Tommy wanted to be famous, a film star, recognised wherever he went; in that regard, Tommy was ambitious. Billy, on the other hand, had no ambitions. He told me he would not amount to much and he achieved just that. Billy was not going to change the world, and would idle away hours in the Lyceum Picture House smoking his Woodbine cigarettes with complete contentment.

Getting away from his rowing family and fighting siblings was his escape route, and in his mind he was up there on the screen with his fictional childhood heroes. Roy Rodgers, the singing cowboy with his horse Trigger; Gene Autry with Champion the Wonder Horse, and of course Audie Murphy knocking shit out of the Germans (again). These were some of Billy's heroes, and Billy was just a simple soul who lived in dreams.

Tommy wanted to make his own dreams come true. However, he was never going to receive an Oscar, attend a premiere or sign an autograph. Nevertheless, Tommy never became bitter. He was not that type of personality and it was just not his style. He was always a kind soul, and if he did get into a rare bad mood, Tommy would paint on a smile. You have to have dreams, thoughts of what you could have been or still could be. It is never too late. Dreams can become reality, but when you leave Shangri–La reality steps back in.

Below the ship, the rudder swivelled and changed our course time and time again below the waves. On board ship, poor Tommy Bryce aka Tommy Twice was a rudderless dreamer. A rudderless dreamer…

Chapter Thirteen

The Entertainer

I WAS ENJOYING myself on the Duke of Rothesay. On board a ship you fall into a routine. It means everyone on board knows what their duties are and are working at their best. The food was good, I had plenty of time off apart from the Scottish Isles and European cruises, and of course during dry dock in Holyhead, Wales, I was home every other day.

Tommy Burke and I shared a cabin. I was on the top bunk, he was on the bottom. We never saw a great deal of each other when we were off duty. When the ship arrived in Heysham, Tommy would finish his shift, and then be off like a shot to see his wife. When the ship arrived in Belfast, I did not hang about either and was off home.

For most of the time everything ran smoothly. With the ship's morning arrival in Belfast, most of the Irish crew would leave for home along with Joe Burn, the Second Chef, who would head for Larne. The Irish crew would then rejoin the ship in the evening. When the ship arrived in Heysham in the morning, the English crew would head for home, some by coach, some by train. They would then rejoin the ship in the evening, the exact same procedure as their Irish shipmates. The exception was Chief Rubin, who had a ten–minute walk to his house as he lived in Heysham itself.

Along with Joe Burns and Old George, I would start to help prepare the food when the ship was lying in Heysham, in between washing the pots and pans. Joe Burns was his usual charismatic self; he seldom spoke a word to me, which was beginning to suit me fine.

Old George was on the ship all of the time. He did not go ashore except on a rare occasion to do a bit of shopping, and curiously he would only go ashore in Belfast. To my knowledge, Old George did not have a home to go to. The ship was his home.

Yes, I was having a good time. I was earning money and buying my own clothes for the first time, enjoying that feeling in life when you can start spending money you have earned. Not having to depend on my parents for clothes was a good feeling: it took pressure off them with their very limited funds, and of course at last I could choose what I wore. That did not mean to say that I knew any better as far as style was concerned: when I was young my mother had a much better idea of what I should wear.

The other good thing about being aboard ship was freedom to a certain extent. No parental control was great because Tom and I were about to sample alcohol for the first time, albeit a very mild light beer.

Jack had already sampled many drinks. We talked to one of the stewards on board ship and asked him if we could buy three bottles of beer. Now the barman was well aware we were all under the legal age to drink alcohol, but he said he would supply us with the beer on the understanding that we would take the bottles straight to our cabins, drink the ale there, dispose of the empty bottles and under no circumstances bother him again. He also said that when we had a taste of the beer we should not have any of the demon drink again, at least until we were of legal age.

It did seem a tad strange to me, when I thought about it over the years, that a chap who made his living from dispensing alcohol would call it the demon drink. He was trying to frighten us without success.

I really was an innocent young lad in so many ways. I remember sitting on my bunk with my first bottle of ale and sipping it very slowly. I tell a lie: I was actually laid down on my bunk because I thought if I get drunk drinking this small bottle of beer I would be laid down anyway and would not fall to the floor.

I was truly an innocent. Every time I thought of this incident through the years it always brought a smile to my face. I also thought that when I got older and started enjoying a drink that if a bottle or two of ale would make me merry then I would be a rich man indeed and have saved myself a hell of a lot of money. Everything in moderation and still have a bloody good time.

Today the trouble is that many people drink at home before they venture out to pubs and nightclubs, and of course they are positively wasted at closing time. Of course, when they awaken the next day they can't remember the night before, but they still tell their friends that they had a wonderful time. They think the more the more alcohol they consume, the better the time they will have, which of course isn't true. The opposite is the truth. I am not preaching, but I would think of my old friend Billy McCann stricken with the disease of alcohol at a very early age, and this always made me sad. Alcoholism is a Belfast disease. It was a terrible blight on some members of my family.

Despite all my gloomy talk about drink, I do enjoy a drink or two, and this enjoyment began that night in Heysham.

I was on my top bunk in my cabin, supping very gingerly on my bottle of ale. Nothing was happening: I was not becoming delirious, I was not drunk and my speech was coherent as I talked to myself. I had not passed out. In fact, I finished the bottle without mishap, and of course I did not fall off my bunk to the floor. In fact, I enjoyed the taste of the ale. We were innocent in those faraway days where stress was an unknown quantity.

With that success under my belt, I had a quick breakfast and went to join my two friends Tom and Jack to see how they had coped with their own little bottle of ale. I met them on deck and they were none the worse for wear.

Tom told me he enjoyed his ale, but Jack did not like his at all and after the first swig he had given his to Tom, which Tom promptly devoured. So Tom had drunk two bottles. We have a piss artist here, I thought to myself

We had a day off to ourselves and decided to walk into Heysham village and catch the bus for Morecambe. A few minutes later we arrived in Heysham and sat down at an old fashioned café.

Much to our surprise and apart from coffee cakes and tea, the owner was serving something in glasses that looked like ginger ale, only he was serving it in wine glasses. I asked him could we have a glass of that ginger ale, and he nearly fell over laughing as he explained that the liquid in the glass was actually home–brewed nettle wine.

Again, to our surprise, he asked us underage fellows if we would like a glass of wine. Tom and I enthusiastically said we would love to; Jack declined the offer. Of course, after our success with the ale, we each managed to down two glasses of that lovely nectar without fright. We thanked the owner and caught the bus for Morecambe.

Whilst wandering along the seafront, a man wearing a pink jacket with a green cravat and carrying a poodle approached us. "Excuse me, but I notice you are sporting a Merchant Navy badge on your blazer," he said to Jack, who told him that the three of us were indeed Merchant Seamen.

He introduced himself (although I subsequently forgot his name) and informed us that he was filming The Entertainer, which was starring his close friend Lawrence Olivier (at that time, 1959, The Entertainer, starring Lawrence Olivier, was indeed being shot in Morecambe).

He went on to tell us that he was the chief cameraman on the film set, and said that if we had time to spare then we could come over that evening to his hotel and he would introduce us to the man himself. We thanked him but hurriedly declined the offer. We weren't used to such gestures, be they genuine or not; a complete stranger approaching complete strangers in the street.

As I was completing this book, and with the wonders of modern technology, I did some research on the internet and recognised the man who had spoken to us that day in photos relating to The Entertainer. He was Denys Coop, a celebrated

British cinematographer, and one of the finest of his generation.

Denys Coop with Laurence Olivier

I suspect now, in the security of that wonderful place called hindsight, that he was genuine and simply making a friendly gesture to some visitors to the area who spoke with a funny accent.

With haste, and back in 1959, Tom, Jack and I made for the bus stop and back to the ship. We had had a good day and met a couple of interesting and diverse personalities.

When I first arrived in England, I soon discovered that people on that side of the Irish Sea were no different from the people on my side of the Irish Sea, back in Belfast where I was born and brought up. The only difference was the different accents, or in other cases, languages. There are good and bad people on this earth and thankfully the bad are a very minute minority.

Chapter Fourteen

Tom and Jerry

TOM AND I soon learned that a few yards from where the ship docked in Heysham harbour was an old railway bridge, and when you walked over that bridge, a few yards from the bottom, there was a decrepit old pub whose appearance was very much in the vein of the decrepit bridge.

Now this was not the sort of place where you would bring your wife or girlfriend. It was what it was: a drinking hole mostly used by the odd docker and certainly by a sailor or two. I don't think any members of the public would have availed themselves of its non–existent pleasures.

I have visited many ports, and have never yet seen a pub that was as close to harbour as this one at Heysham. Over a rickety bridge and you were there. But even though the ships were invitingly close to this pub, I never heard of any drunken seaman falling into the waters at the dockside, and believe me they could drink: you could see one or two of them perilously close to disaster but yet they always avoided a soaking.

This was a pub on your doorstep, convenient and tempting when you were off duty. Jack and I started going over on occasion, and rough and ready as the pub was, and rough and ready as the landlord was, he would not serve us alcohol, neither did we expect him to: we were underage and quite content to drink our lemonade and orange. We were here for the floor show: to watch them getting drunk, the odd fight, and the landlord ejecting a few from time to time.

Some regulars for a time were two Belfast blokes who were never thrown out by the landlord because they could hold their drink, and believe me they could drink them all under the table. Jack and I would watch with wonder as these two guys, who visited the pub about twice a week, would drink literally gallons of the black liquid and walk out of there with a steady gait and unquivering word.

Pat Gibson and Joe Lanigan were stewards who waited on tables quite competently. They had to work together, and got on well when they were working. The problem was that when they got the drink down them their personalities changed completely and they took on different personas.

Joe Lanigan was a tall, well–built guy and a bad one with the drink. Pat Gibson, on the other hand, was smaller in stature, not a bad lad, and took the mickey out of Lanigan relentlessly: that is where the trouble lay. Pat liked to take the piss, Lanigan did not like the piss taken, and that is how the chase always began.

The first I knew about them was when I had been on the ship about a week. We were lying in Heysham and it was about three o'clock in the afternoon. Most of the crew were taking it easy, having a lie down and getting charged up for the start of work in the evening before the passengers would start to embark. Not Pat and Lanigan; no, they did not rest. As soon as these two sweethearts exited the drinking hole after last orders, the chase started.

Pat Gibson always left before Joe Lanigan; this gave him a bit of a head start. Lanigan always kept Gibson in his sights as soon as they left the pub, and as soon as Pat Gibson walked on the gangplank, Lanigan started running. I know this for a fact, because Jack and I decided to hang on until they both departed the pub and saw before our eyes the beginning of the chase.

One afternoon I was stood in the galley enjoying a cup of

tea and a sandwich . This was a lovely time for me as there was no one around, no hustle and bustle of crew: complete peace and quiet. Quite suddenly, and without warning, Pat Gibson shoots past me like a rat up a drainpipe, followed about five seconds later by a gust of wind in the shape of Joe Lanigan. Gibson had exited the pantry department which is adjacent to the galley and was on the port deck when Lanigan entered the galley fuming and swearing really loud:

"Stop you little Fenian bastard!" His shouting terrified me: it was not a sight you often saw. When I collected my senses afterwards, an ironic smile came to my face as I recalled with amusement what Lanigan shouted to Gibson: they were both Catholics.

There was a hell of a difference in their physical appearances, too. Pat Gibson was slim and stood five foot six with high heels, while Joe Lanigan was well built and stood six foot two without high heels. Even today I can never understand why they acted like this on such a frequent basis. But the scary thing is that to my knowledge they never actually came to blows, probably because Pat Gibson was far too fast for his adversary, and of course fatigue set in after a few moments into the chase, and they retired to their respective cabins; the drink did tell after a while.

Of course, Pat Gibson was always wary, took no chances and locked himself in the cabin. Their behaviour and routines were bizarre, but through the years I did laugh whenever I recalled it. When they did finally meet up, it was always in the evening, when they were dressed up, shining clean and ready for work. What with The Bungalow to come and Phil Lavery the bad guy, as well as Tommy Bryce who was Tommy Twice, these were two real dears; life was never going to be boring in the Merchant Navy.

Pat Gibson and Joe Lanigan reminded me of two of my favourite cartoon characters, Tom and Jerry: Tom Cat and Jerry Mouse. They made me laugh and forget my troubles when I was growing up on a ship away from home and surrounded by the wide, fickle sea.

Chapter Fifteen

Sailing The Blues

I MET AND came across quite a few diverse characters while I was in the Merchant Navy, ranging from the slightly unhinged to the eccentric, the definitely strange to the almost completely happy. A broad range of the human species, it was no different from civvy street; the only difference was that outside the Navy you can walk or run away. Not so when you are at sea: there you have a captive audience, and the audience holds you captive.

Even aboard the Duke of Rothesay which was a coastal vessel, a short trip across the Irish Sea could be enlightening, even entertaining. On board a ship which travels the world upon the deep sea, you can be on the ocean for days and weeks. There is no escape, as I would later discover…

Two characters I came across fell under the categories that I have mentioned; one was strange, another almost completely happy. I met Bill Turner and wish that I had not: he was the strange one. The other was called just Tommy and I did not meet him, I just heard him: Tommy was a singer. These two characters were chalk and cheese; worlds apart.

On about my fourth day on board ship a strange man

approached me. The ship had just docked in Heysham. It was a bright sunny morning, most of the passengers had disembarked and a few in the first class restaurant were finishing their breakfast. Overall, things had quietened down. In the galley, food was being put back in the fridge; the pots and pans had been washed and stored away. Tommy Burke the chef had retired to his cabin to wash and change and head for home. I was stood in the galley with old George and we were enjoying a mug of well–earned tea.

"Good morning!" I heard someone bellow. I looked around and this dapper little man was approaching me. "Good morning!" rang in my ears again and at the same time a card was shoved into my free hand. He beamed at me. "I'm your union rep!"

"What are you...?" I replied. I was not expecting this encounter so early in the morning. I must admit that I was taken by surprise: I did not know what a union rep was as I had never heard the term before.

"I'm your union rep!" he bellowed once more. "I'm here to welcome you into the Seafarers' Union. That means we look after your interests and most importantly we make sure your employers look after your interests. I collect union dues every month. Nice to welcome you into our union!" And he was gone.

I turned to Old George. "Who is he?"

"He's the union rep," Old George replied. "He will look after you. We are all in the union on board ship." Old George was obviously a fan of Bill Turner.

We went on strike once from the Duke of Rothesay while it sat in Belfast. Tommy Burke told me to go home. I did. But what it was all about, I did not have a clue, and no one was about to explain to me, a mere youth, what the cause was. I certainly never noticed any difference in my pay and conditions. So that was that, a brief encounter with Bill Turner, a land lubber who came under my definition of a strange person.

Tommy was a passenger and a singer. He travelled on the ship about every fortnight. He joined the ship in Belfast, stayed somewhere in England or so I was told, and travelled back to Belfast.

I first heard Tommy before I saw him. I had finished my

duties in the galley on that particular evening and was taking my usual stroll around the ship. As I was passing the lounge, I heard this guitar being strummed and someone singing. I looked in and saw this young chap wearing a cowboy hat and singing the blues. That is, he was singing a Tommy Steele song popular at the time, called "Singing the Blues." I started talking to one of the barmen who served drinks in the lounge. He told me that Tommy was a regular passenger who sets up his guitar around eight thirty to nine o'clock and starts singing, and 'by the way that good looking girl sat beside him is his girlfriend.'

About half an hour into his routine, he takes his hat off, sets it beside the girl and before long people start putting money into it. Luke the deckhand came to join me and went on to tell me that when Tommy started singing he always kept his hat on. Probably one reason for that was because he was going bald.

We noticed the state of his scalp one night because for the first time he took his hat off as it was an extremely hot and humid night. He could not believe his luck, for as soon as he put his hat beside his lovely girlfriend, one or two passengers started putting coins into it. So from that moment on, that fortunate moment on, Tommy would take his hat off a few minutes after he had started singing.

"What's his real name?" I asked Luke.

"I haven't a clue, nor has anyone else," he replied.

The reason people started calling him Tommy was because most of his repertoire was made up of Tommy Steele songs. Tommy Steele at that time was a very popular pop star. Tommy sang the odd Cliff Richard song but most of the time his songs were from his own albums.

The Tommy on board our ship was a singer, a troubadour, an almost completely happy fellow and, I believe, the first busker I ever saw. I had already met a few diverse characters and this was only my first ship. I did not know it then, but I would meet many more. I was sixteen then, and on that night I believe my childhood ended, although I never gave that date any great thought at the time.

Dates are of no consequence; just scratchings on a rock which is roasted by the sun or bombarded by the ocean waves.

Chapter Sixteen

The Sea and I

ONE DAY, I decided that I needed a break. I had just experienced a terribly rough crossing, to put it mildly. The Irish Sea had told us once again that she is in command! She dictates the weather.

I had only been in the Merchant Navy a few short months, and had already experienced a few rough crossings from Belfast to Heysham, although this one was the most frightening. The oceans and the seas cannot be conquered, and this particular sea had thrown us about and there was nothing we could do about it.

It was like a ghost ship: passengers were stumbling along the decks like zombies. It was extremely difficult to keep your balance, to keep yourself from falling and injuring yourself. It has always fascinated me why some people will try and keep their balance in rough seas on board a ship. The passengers with common sense will get off the deck and into shelter: in the lounge, in the bar, anywhere inside, and if you have a cabin all the better reason for bedding down in some comfort. But common sense is not so common.

Winter gales can blow through the Irish Sea faster than a

freight train, and they are unpredictable. Tonight was such a night. A benign Irish Sea can suddenly turn nasty and leave you unprepared. Sometimes the deck crew especially can be taken by surprise, and conditions can be very testing. There was vomit all over the ship's decks, and the passengers that could make it in time were hanging over the ship's rails, spewing their waste into the ruthless sea. Any seagulls that were around (and there are always some no matter the weather) were not treating themselves to this vomit before it hit the waves. As I have confessed, the sight of these passengers looking bedraggled and wishing they were somewhere else, anywhere but on this ship, did bring a chuckle to my face.

When I first joined my ship we had had a rough crossing during which I had eaten a chocolate ice cream, although it did not stay down in my stomach very long. It caught me by surprise, came up straightaway out of my mouth and all over my clothes; but from that moment on, the seas or the oceans never caught me out again! That is why I was having a quiet laugh and feeling victorious, watching these poor wretches being sick, dazed and completely disorientated.

I decided to go inside. I visited the bar first, where a couple of hardy souls sat their pints of the black stuff gripped tightly in their hands. These two were not giving up their pints of Guinness to the sea. I was quite surprised that the bar was still open, but when I had a closer look I saw that the shutters were firmly closed.

My next location was the lounge. The lounge was massive: plenty of room for everyone. Every sofa and chair was occupied. People were laid out everywhere and there was not an empty sofa or chair. People were trying without much success to sleep. It was a scene of carnage, with sick all over the carpets. The lucky, more affluent or simply wiser passengers who had booked cabins were tucked up safely in their beds. The stewards and stewardesses were going to have their work cut out in the morning when the ship docked.

I looked into a couple of toilets: a terrible sight. Again, people were being sick or had been sick, and I stayed by the door; no way was I entering. I could see that the floors were slippery from vomit, and the smell was stomach churning. I made a hasty exit and retreated to my cabin. I would have to be up the next morning to prepare breakfast, although I believed that only the hardiest of passengers would be partaking of this meal. So I decided there and then a few days holiday were due me. I would put in for four or five days' leave and try and meet up with a friend or two, although I had not seen many people I knew when I was home every other day.

When I did come home, and by the time I had sorted out my laundry, bought a few things, had long chats with my mother and father and seen the odd aunt and uncle, had a cup of tea and answered their questions about life on board ship, I did not have any time to spare before I joined my ship again. So this holiday would perhaps give me time to see a few old friends.

I would never forget the haphazard crossing of the Irish Sea that I had experienced on that particular crossing, and it reminded me once again that the sea is master of all.

Chapter Seventeen

Short Break

MY **HOLIDAY STARTED**. Dirty laundry to Ma; she will wash, iron and fold neatly for me. I had a piece of toast, mug of tea and a long chat with Ma: she liked bringing me up to date with everything. Then I headed off up my little street, Singleton Street, and onto the New Lodge Road.

Just as I entered the road I heard this almighty shout followed by a piercing wolf whistle. I turned round to see one of my old mates, Sean Connolly, coming towards me.

"That was a lovely wolf whistle, Sean. Do you fancy me, then?" I said.

"Very funny, Kenny," Sean replied. "If I don't find a girlfriend soon I will have to start fancying somebody. Anyway, joking aside you look bloody well, Kenny; the Merchant Navy is good for you."

"How come, Sean, I am home every other day and I never see you? Or come to think of it, why don't I see any of my old friends?"

"Well," Sean replied, "as you know Jerry Wilson and his family have immigrated to Canada, the drink has done for Billy

McCann, and the rest of the crew are working. I don't see them very often myself, Kenny."

Sean went on to tell me that had started work as an apprentice plumber a few months ago and was knackered most of the time.

"Anyway," he added, "what was stopping you calling on me?"

I had no answer for that one.

We walked up the New Lodge Road towards Lynch's pub and there standing on the corner was Soldier Brown. Soldier was an infantryman in the Army. He had signed up for twenty two years and told us he loved it. He was stationed in Germany, had travelled quite a bit and was now a lance corporal. He came home from time to time to keep his fretting Ma happy; otherwise he said he would not bother.

Soldier then suggested we partake of some lunchtime refreshment in the pub. Sean squirmed at this suggestion.

"I'm not allowed to drink; my Ma and Da would kill me if they smelled booze on me."

"That's alright," Soldier bellows sarcastically. "Run along home and we will see you later."

We entered the pub. I had been here twice before with my eldest brother Fred, who had treated me to a half pint of Guinness which I must confess I rather enjoyed. The landlord never batted an eyelid when Fred ordered a drink for me. My eldest brother Fred was a frequent visitor to Lynch's and knew I would be no trouble.

The strange thing is that I was just seventeen years old and should not be in a pub drinking alcohol. I still do not understand to this day why the landlord tolerated me drinking in his pub when I was under the legal age; it was not lemonade or orange I was supping: it was alcohol.

Soldier had been drinking alcohol since he was about fourteen years old, but not in a pub of course. His father kept a little cellar of booze in the house: lager, cider, Guinness, of course, and a wine rack full of bottles.

When his Da and Ma went out shopping or to see friends, Soldier would start sampling some of the booze. This went on for quite a while, and his father didn't seem to notice the odd bottle of Guinness or lager missing. It was only when Soldier decided to treat himself to the wine that his father noticed the dwindling stock: Mr. Brown's collection of wine was his pride and joy. He admonished his son, put a lock on the cellar door and from that moment on Soldier was deprived of his illicit booze.

Soldier had dreamt of joining the army ever since he was a little boy, and when he came of age his father could not wait to get him down to that recruiting office. Soldier would not let me get my hand in my pocket to buy a drink; he said it was on him.

When the pub was getting ready to close, I had had two half pints of Guinness to Soldier's three pints of Guinness and three whisky chasers. That man could bloody drink! I was not going to drink any more.

I had to sneak into my house, sneak into the parlour and hope that my Ma could not hear or see me. Just like Sean Connolly's Ma, my Ma, not to mention my Da, would certainly not tolerate my drinking. I bought a packet of strong mints in the shop to sweeten my breath and hopefully disguise the smell of booze, I shook hands with Soldier and said we would meet tomorrow; he was due to fly back to Germany the next day.

We did not meet the next day.

We never saw each other again. But we had departed the best of friends, as ever we were.

Chapter Eighteen

Loves Lost

I WAS INTO the third day of my short break: two days to go. Apart from Sean and Soldier, I never caught the slightest glimpse of any of my old childhood mates. I suppose that they, like me, were growing up, had left school and childhood behind and were now working, which in itself was a miracle because jobs were few and far between.

Almost everyone without exception had to leave school and try to find work, any work, and beggars cannot be choosers. Those one or two around our way with aspirations to go on to university would have to put their plans on hold.

Every family that I knew of with two exceptions were poor. There was no shame in being poor as everyone was in the same boat. And we may have been poor, but in those days we could laugh, and we felt in those bleak days that you can't look forward when you are always looking back. In spite of our hardships, we tried to hold firm to this conviction.

On my last day ashore, I got up early, had a hearty breakfast and decided to go for a long walk. I walked down the New Lodge Road, North Queen Street, York Street, then on to the

Shore Road and turned left on to Fort William Park. I walked up the length of Fort William, turned left on to the Antrim Road, turned left back on to the New Lodge Road and into my little Singleton Street and home.

Just in time for lunch. Stew, to be exact.

New Lodge Road and Antrim Road

In the last couple of days I had passed the fruit and vegetable shop that belonged to Annie Hughes several times. I had looked through the shop window but there was no sign of Annie. One of the things I had wanted to do on my break was to see Annie again. As a young boy, I had admired Annie from afar and had appreciated her beauty. The few times I had spoken to her I was shy and tongue tied. Throughout my childhood and teenage years the sight of Annie had seldom left my thoughts: a young boy's infatuation. Annie was in her thirties and when I had last seen her was still a lovely prospect to behold: a beautiful sight for young eyes sore with longing and hormones.

I told my Ma that I had passed Annie's shop a few times and seen not a sign of her. Straightaway my Ma told me that Annie had sold her shop and moved away; no one knew where. I asked my Ma why she had moved; it was clear to all that she loved that shop.

My mother went on to tell me that Annie gave short shrift

to men, for whom she had no time, and as everyone suspected, her shop assistant Olive was Annie's love and that Annie was Olive's love. They were seen out on several occasions, openly holding hands and kissing.

My mother said that one day, about a month ago, they had had this terrible row which ended up in the street. After that almighty row, which a few people had witnessed, Olive was never seen again.

Annie started drinking heavily; she always liked her drink, but this time she was putting it down her in huge amounts. My mother said as soon as you walked in the shop you could smell the alcohol, and that Annie's speech was slurred and she stumbled about the shop.

In a relatively short space of time Annie had become almost obese; this once slim, laughing woman had become bloated and fat. What I gathered from my mother's recollection was that Annie could only walk with great difficulty; the burden of her flesh made it impossible for her to walk even a short distance; all this decline and unhappiness came about with a terrible swiftness.

This revelation really saddened me and left me with a heavy heart: this handsome woman had intrigued me. Sometimes true love, or what we think it is, does not always run smooth; young love, old love, any love in any form, and when this happens it is of course devastating. This is what Annie experienced, in the most terrible and traumatic way and it broke the poor woman's heart.

The last time I saw Annie, she was a vision of loveliness stood before me, wrapped up in a lovely fresh cotton dress.

That is how I will always see Annie.

Chapter Nineteen

Beth

THE LAST DAY of my short break. The following evening I would be joining my ship. My childhood crush, my fantasy of Annie, had come to an abrupt end. My one consolation was my Ma telling me that under no circumstances was Annie interested in boys or men. This softened the blow.

My other consolation was that Ms. Hughes was light years ahead of me in age. Little did I know that another crush was about to come into my life, quite unexpectedly and suddenly.

I had a bit of breakfast and went for my usual constitutional but once again did not see anyone I knew. I arrived back at home just before lunch; I always did time that well. I let myself in the house; our front door was seldom locked, something hard to contemplate nowadays. I walked up the little hall past the little parlour where I heard my Ma engaged in conversation.

This was not unusual in our house. My Ma was a very sociable lady; she invited everyone into our house to have a natter, and even the odd stray was refreshed with a cup of tea.

I went into the kitchen and was about to put the kettle on for a cup of tea, when my Ma shouted for me to come into the parlour. I entered the parlour and was confronted by this lovely sight before me: a ginger–haired, slightly freckled, pretty young girl. She took my breath away for a few seconds.

As my eyes were going back into their sockets, my Ma began to introduce me.

"Kenny, this is Beth; Beth, this is my son, Kenny."

Simple introduction.

We both nervously said hello to each other. Mother went on to tell me that Beth lived a few streets down from us, and that her father, Mr. McManus, ran the butchers shop on the New Lodge Road. I was hooked straight away.

I was not a man of the world: I had not long entered the age of seventeen and no romantic liaisons had come my way. I was extremely naïve as regards the female species; an awkward boy, timid and bloody daft. My heart was skipping a few beats before this young girl.

We had a cup of tea and a sandwich, and with all the courage I could muster, when Beth was ready to go, I offered to walk her home and perhaps meet her tomorrow before I joined my ship. To my surprise she agreed to this and I walked her the short distance to her father's shop. Her family lived above the shop.

I said cheerio and with a spring in my step and a slight bravado skipped back to my house. And then I thought to myself that I bet my Ma had deliberately planned a meeting between Beth and me. My mother was a natural matchmaker, always trying to fix people up: boy meets girl.

It would not be the first time that she had engaged in such romantic diplomacy. Whatever her motive, I was extremely pleased that she had put this lovely young thing in our parlour. This was a lovely ending to my short break, and my only regret was that I had not met her at the start of my holiday, or months before for that matter.

"Why, why, why?" said the voice in my head.

For the last three or four months I had been thinking that it was time for me to start making plans to leave the Duke of Rothesay. I was getting itchy feet. I wanted to go deep sea. I wanted to see new countries.

As planned, Beth came to our house and talked with Ma for a while. I wondered what their conversation was about. Beth and I then went for a walk. As you do, we talked about everything and nothing. I told her about life on board my ship; she told me about her plans to go to college and become a nurse. We ended our walk at her house above the butcher's shop. I said hello to her Ma and Da; we departed saying we would meet as often as we could when my ship was in Belfast.

We did meet again and saw each other about twice a week. Our pleasures were simple: we went on walks and visited the Lyceum Picture House at the top of the New Lodge Road. We were really adventurous in those days. A peck on the cheek eventually led to the kissing of each other's lips, and that is as far as it went. Innocent times.

Always on the back of my mind was the thought of foreign travel; in fact, I thought about it almost every day, which slightly complicated matters because I was thinking of Beth almost every day too. Yet the lure of foreign travel was starting to win the battle.

I had been walking out with Beth for about a month, when a shipmate who knew of my plans to leave the Duke of Rothesay told me to get down to the Merchant Navy pool. He said a couple of ships were due in Belfast in the next week or so and were looking for crew.

"Get down there," he said, "and put your name down; tell them to keep you in mind if any catering vacancies were being advertised."

There is a Merchant Navy pool or office established in all the main ports. It is a building where merchant seamen gather to see what ships are in port and if they are employing; the maritime equivalent of an employment exchange. I did go, and told them that I had been promoted recently to the position of assistant cook on my present ship, and would be interested in any ship that was going deep sea.

A couple of days later I was talking to Tommy McGee who was still courting my eldest sister, Mary, and I was extremely glad that he was because when I told him of my plans to leave my present ship and hopefully go deep sea, he said no problem. Tommy had fixed me up with my present position, and said he would keep his eye open and let me know what ships were coming into Belfast and if they had any positions available.

I was glad I had mentioned this to Tommy: I had a feeling in my water that things would soon be changing and I had complete faith in this man. Who needed the Merchant Navy establishment when you had fellas like Tommy McGee on board? He was a one-man employment exchange, a one-stop shop to get this boy on a ship out of Belfast again.

So there I was, old Kenny boy seeing a pretty girl and a chance to shortly go on foreign travels. Of course, at that time the thought never entered my head that foreign travels would mean the end of pretty Beth, or maybe not. Perhaps Beth would wait for me. We would have to wait and see.

I was getting ahead of myself. Whatever the outcome, the idea of travelling far and wide, of seeing new, faraway places was taking over my thoughts, night and day, day and night. I went to my bed that night a very happy young fella.

Chapter Twenty

Nearly There

ABOUT TWO WEEKS after I had mentioned my plans to Tommy, he informed me of a foreign–going ship called the Inishowen Head, which would sail into Belfast within a couple of days. He told me that this particular vessel made six–week trips. He did not mention destinations and I did not press him; for the time being that was not important.

The ship would be in dry dock for an overhaul and would probably be laid up for at least a month.

"I know most of the officers on the ship," Tommy told me. He would have a word, get me an informal interview with the first officer, and hopefully the chief cook would be there too. "As long as you look tidy, present yourself well, then everything should be fine," Tommy reassured me. "There is vacancy for an assistant cook, and you have recently been promoted, so I don't see any problems."

Tommy departed, telling me not worry, the job was mine. I did trust him: Tommy knew everyone from the Harbour Master to the ships' crews down to the dockers and the checkers. He had fixed me up with my first ship, the Duke of Rothesay, and was about to fix me up with my second ship, the Inishowen Head.

As long as he was courting my sister and she was keeping him sweet, Tommy McGee would be my unofficial, unpaid employment agent.

About three days after the Inishowen Head had arrived in Belfast, Tommy called for me to come with him to the ship which was not lying far from where "my" ship, the Duke of Rothesay, was docked. I had a quick look at the vessel and quickly concluded that it had seen better days. This ship was going into dry dock for overhaul and not before time.

We walked on board and were met straightaway by the Second Officer who introduced himself. He in turn brought us to the galley where we met the chef. We shook hands and exchanged a few words. The chef nodded to the Second Officer who told me the job was for me. Just like that!

The position of assistant cook on board the Inishowen Head was mine. Like a secret club. A minimum of words. A handshake and the job was fixed.

Tommy must have done all the ground work the day before. I would assume that the Merchant Navy is today much more stringent, strict and selective than what it was back then.

I felt pretty good with myself although I returned to reality with a jolt when I remembered that I would have to tell everybody about my plans. I did think it was strange that in all my nervousness in meeting the Second Officer and chef I did not have a good look at the galley where I would be spending most of my time. That evening, before I joined my ship, I told my Ma and Da the news. I told them that I was leaving the Duke of Rothesay, would be joining the Inishowen Head in a few weeks and would be heading abroad for long stretches. Their reaction was what I expected.

"Good for you, well done, and just be careful in foreign lands." My parents never discouraged me in any way; they were always behind me, whatever course I decided to take.

My next step was to inform Chief Steward Rubin of my intention to leave. The Second Officer of the Inishowen Head had informed me that all going well the ship would be departing in a month's time and that I should report for duty in three weeks' time. He gave me the day and date. I gave Rubin two weeks' notice, hoping that that would be enough. Much to my relief he told me that that was fine. I secretly believed that one day's notice would have sufficed.

Rubin had made no secret of the fact that his wife was on his back frequently to get her two sisters' boys fixed up with jobs. My leaving would suit him just well and of course keep his wife happy for a while. I need not have worried, and am now sure that Rubin was relieved and glad to be seeing the back of me.

The strange thing is, amongst all the excitement of joining a new ship, I had no idea where the vessel would be heading. My mind began to guess at all the possible locations around the world it might be taking me.

Back in Belfast I sought out Tommy who told me that the ship went on six or seven long week voyages. He informed me that the ship travelled to Galveston, in Texas, and that it stopped at Le Havre to pick up cargo. That part never interested me; I just wanted to know the destinations. The return journey was the reverse, Tommy told me she departs Texas, on to Le Havre where she discharges her cargo, or part of it, and finally back to Belfast. After a couple of days she would start the same journey again.

"Brilliant," I exclaimed with a forced bravado, before an awareness of the distances assailed my brain. "Bloody hell, Tommy; that is a long way away from my house in Belfast."

I would not be crossing the Irish Sea again in the near future. This time I would be crossing the Atlantic Ocean.

81

Chapter Twenty One

Cheerio

MY FAMILY KNEW of my plans to leave the Duke of Rothesay in two weeks' time. The only member of the ship's crew who knew I would be leaving was Rubin the Chief Steward. He was delighted I was leaving but kept it well hidden. He was quite happy to see anyone go as long as it was not him, and could now get part of his family aboard.

That evening, leaving Belfast, I told Tommy Burke and Old George in the galley that I had given my notice and that I would be leaving in a fortnight. They were surprised to say the least.

"Are you taking the piss, lad?" was Tommy's first input, "I thought you were happy here, Ken."

"I am happy here, Tommy," I replied, "but I've had a yearning to go deep sea for a while now and travel a bit, see a foreign country or two."

"Well, that's alright! Quite understandable, young man," he replied.

"We shall miss him George," said Tommy. Old George nodded agreement with a twinkle in his eye, and smiling, replied: "We will that."

I would certainly miss these two men: they were work mates, ship mates, but more than that they had been good friends to me. Tommy Burke had been my mentor, my teacher and my guardian. He was a good, solid man. Old George was eccentric, delightful, scruffy, humorous and always smiling, and a joy to work with; of course, he was also my teacher. In spite of his length of years the old fellow never complained. He tolerated, with good humour, this young upstart from Crumlin. All these years later when I look back, an image of Old George has always made me chuckle with glee: his shuffling along in the galley with old, dilapidated slippers on his feet. He gave up asking why I always had a smile on my face when he appeared in his torn cardigan and with a dirty old mug that he seldom had out of his hand and always full of tea.

When I joined the Duke of Rothesay and started work in the galley, Joe Burns, the second cook, was the opposite of Tommy and Old George. Sullen and unsociable, he told me from the very start to watch and learn, but never to bother him. And I never did! I would be glad to see the back of him.

I would also miss Tom and Jack, my old pals: we had had some fun together and they would really be sorry to see me go. But I knew they would not be long in following me and going deep sea.

The Duke of Rothesay had been good for me. I had enjoyed myself tremendously and had met a whole range of people: the good, the bad and the ugly. I had learnt how to cook, how to look after myself and interact with people. My boyhood country shyness was nearly behind me. I had already travelled extensively: a short cruise round the Scottish islands, followed by a European cruise in which I had visited a few cities in different countries.

Now I was about to embark on a completely new adventure, crossing the Atlantic ocean to America. During the few days remaining before joining the Inishowen Head, I was feeling slightly nervous, but that feeling left me soon enough and before long I was thinking of the adventure before me and, of course, of seeing America. That land where so many Irish went, one way or another; some to return, some to stay, some to disappear without a trace from history. That land where our heroes in the films came from.

Hold on, though. In all this excitement, and unbelievably, I had not even thought of Beth. How could this be? Beth was no longer a crush: I was in love, I loved her. Or so I thought. It was, I suppose, and would turn out to be, an infatuation, puppy love. Nevertheless, we enjoyed each other's company, and so to me, unworldly youth that I was, that was love. Yet I could not believe that Beth had not entered my thoughts at this particular time.

My ship had already left Belfast that evening. I determined that I would see her as soon as the ship docked in Belfast the following day. How could I have not told this pretty young thing my plans before I had told so many others? The following day, a couple of hours after we had docked, I called for Beth. It was a Saturday, so I knew she would be at home. I knocked at her door; she answered. We greeted, we walked, we talked, we kissed. I then broke news of my plans gently. I told her that I was leaving the Duke of Rothesay, joining a new ship called the Inishowen Head, and whispered softly that this ship was foreign going and I would be leaving on it to travel to Le Havre and then on to Galveston, Texas. America.

It was very dramatic. Everything was going alright until I mentioned America: this threw her completely. She was extremely shocked to say the least and a few tears gathered in her eyes.

"But Ken, we have only been walking out together for a few short weeks, and you are going to leave me."

"But not for long," I hastily said, "Only for six or seven weeks."

"That is a long time to me," Beth replied. She collected her thoughts. "Will you think of me when you are away, Ken? Will you, Ken...?" Before I could reply, Beth retorted, "Because I will think of you every day, Ken. No, I will think of you every hour."

"Of course I will think of you every hour, every day! You will be in my thoughts constantly."

So with our solemn promises cemented, we agreed that in the next few days we would see each other every other day when the ship and I were in Belfast. The day before I was leaving to join The Inishowen Head we said our tearful farewells, promised our undying love, and swore that we would never part.

Chapter Twenty Two

I'm Off

IN SEPTEMBER 1959 for the second time, I stepped on to the gangplank of the Inishowen Head, only this time I would be a member of the crew. I had worked my two weeks' notice on the Duke of Rothesay, said my goodbyes to my friends and workmates and to my Ma and Da and family. Last but not least I said a special farewell to Beth, my first love.

I had a bad feeling about this ship as soon as I had stepped on board. That gut feeling, that deep sense that something is not quite right, although at the time you cannot quite put your finger on it or explain it.

I was shown to my cabin by the only steward on board ship, a bit of a dogsbody really. It was a small cabin where indeed a cat could not be swung, and was in a bad state of repair. The mattress was thin and lumpy, and covered with a sheet. The only thing that cheered me up about it was the fact that I was not sharing. Two people in that cabin would have been overcrowding. So my quarters were my first disappointment.

The steward brought me up to the galley to once again meet the chef, who informed me that we would be sitting in Belfast harbour for at least a week due to last minute repairs and a late cargo arriving. He went on to tell me that this would give the steward and me time to give the galley an overhaul.

I wondered what exactly he meant, but after having my first good look at the surroundings, I thought it was long overdue. The steward and I would be spending the next few days cleaning. The chef would be doing the bulk of the cooking, but as I discovered, only until the galley was brought up to a good state of cleanliness.

On the captain's orders, there would be no shore leave for anyone. This didn't bother me as I considered this as the beginning of the voyage. The next few days were spent scrubbing, cleaning, washing and mopping. The steward and I were completely knackered. It was an old ship, with an old galley, but when we had finished at least it was clean, hygienic and fit for purpose.

After ten days, cargo loaded, last minute repairs completed and everything shipshape, we set sail for the port of Le Havre. It was a slow, overnight sailing. I had another bad feeling when the chef explained to me after we had set sail for France that I would be up early to prepare and cook breakfast and to serve it to the crew, and of course clean the pots and pans afterwards. Then prepare lunch and help to cook it with him. He would prepare and cook dinner. That was good of him, I thought to myself.

Hold on a minute: I am washing pots and pans and doing most of the cooking.

It dawned on me that we did not have a galley boy: I am the galley boy as well as the assistant cook. I thought that I had finished cleaning cooking utensils when I was promoted to assistant cook. I also thought it strange, and wondered why I had not noticed before, that this ship did not have a galley boy. The company was obviously cutting down on costs, and this lazy sod was having a laugh at my expense.

Now I had an idea why they had hired me at a moment's notice with a nod and a wink and not a proper chat. The reason was I suspected they would not get an experienced cook, a seasoned cook, an older cook, because he probably would have asked a few questions, had a good look around and then turned the position down flat. That is why I got the job without any fuss.

We docked in Le Havre in the early morning and started taking on more cargo. We would be here for two days. This captain did not seem to be in any hurry at all. Since joining this ship I was completely exhausted. I began to think a return voyage to The United States of America was not for me after all, and started to think of ways of abandoning this tug boat. Apart from that, I was the only crew member who was in their teens; all the crew members looked to me like they had passed their sell-by date. I was feeling cut off and lonely.

Then there was the chef. Well, he was not a chef, and I use that term lightly. He might just have cut it as a glorified cook. To add to that he was bad company and a lazy bastard.

No, after much soul searching, I gave credence to the thought that this ship and I would have to part company, and part company before she headed for Texas.

Apart from anything else, I was lovesick and homesick after only a few days on board this barge, and just knew deep down that a few weeks away would not be prudent or wise.

A lot of the trouble was down to life on board. There was no company for a young lad, the chef was a miserable bugger, the cabin was a shithole and the work was a bloody slog. At times I seemed to be the only one cooking and the chef skived off as often as he could. I would not be caught again like this, I told myself, a resolution to which I intended to remain firm.

I was missing Beth and I hoped she was missing me, and suffering from that adult affliction known as homesickness: that need, deep down in your belly, running throughout your soul, to get back home just as soon as you possibly could and to hell with rhyme and reason.

Chapter Twenty Three

Seul

MY **MIND WAS** made up. I had given it much thought and finally decided that this tug boat and I should part company. One of the reasons for my decision to quit this vessel was the state of the ship itself.

It had been in dry dock, undergoing extensive overhaul, and whilst the outer shell was spic and span, the inner had been sadly neglected. Another reason was the so–called cook: he was a lazy bastard. I was doing all the work and that was before the ship had even left Belfast. I would have weeks of early mornings, busy breakfasts and lunches, before that idle sod would present himself.

That was bad enough, but I would be washing pots and pans and mopping the galley deck. I thought I had left that all behind when I had been promoted to cook. Enough is enough, I told myself. But the overriding decision to head for the exit was Beth: I just could not stop thinking about her, and the thought of a few weeks away was too long and too much to bear. I was well and truly hooked.

On the second day in Le Havre the ship was preparing to leave at approximately noon. I finished breakfast and started to prepare lunch. I then went to the cook's cabin (I never did get his name), told him that I would be going ashore to post a letter, and would only be a few minutes. I told him that I would finish lunch preparation when I came back. He gave his usual nod and told me not to hang about. I did not.

I dashed back to my cabin, had a quick wash, put on my civvy trousers, a shirt and jumper and jacket. All I had brought on board when I joined the ship was what I was wearing to go ashore.

I took an envelope from my drawer, put a blank piece of paper in, wrote my home address and sealed it. I made my way up on deck and walked to the gangplank. The third officer was on duty there.

"Where are you going, Cook?" he casually asked. I waved the letter in his face and told him I was going to the post office to post it. I said it was very important. "We are sailing in two hours, so hurry back!"

"No problem, I can speak a little French, so I won't be too long."

"Clever you, speaking French," he replied. This did reassure him, although he really did not seem too concerned whether I hurried back or not. He had more important things to attend to.

Of course, I could not speak a word of French, but at the time it did not concern me, such as I was obsessed with getting of that ship.

Earlier I had prepared a couple of sandwiches and had a small bottle of water tucked in my coat so I would not go hungry or thirsty if the course of my stay in Le Havre was not prolonged.

I must admit that when I walked down the gang plank for the last time, and on to land, it dawned on me that I really was on my own. Alone: I had never been alone, really alone. I had grown up in a small house with several siblings and hardly a second of solitude. This was the first time that I was going to be on my own since leaving the cradle and not only that: I was in a foreign land, and not able to speak their language. That was when I started to feel a little apprehensive, a little nervous and a little scared.

Be careful what you wish for.

I walked around Le Havre, for about two hours. I never strayed too far from the harbour. The Inishowen Head was due to leave at noon, and that was about now. I wandered towards the spot where the ship was docked, obviously keeping my head down. To my surprise the tug boat was moving. She was on her way. She was leaving on time; this really surprised me. She was setting sail for America, without me, and that did please me. But the thought struck me again: you are on your own in a foreign country, Kenny boy!

I was reassured by the fact that I knew enough to know that there was a British Consul in Le Havre and that they would hopefully arrange for my passage home. I had a sandwich, a drink, and started to ask people passing by the directions to the British Consulate; none of them could speak English, and I could not speak French, so it was hard work.

It was coming up to early evening, the daylight would soon be disappearing and I was becoming very concerned when I spotted a Gendarme, the first one all day.

Please speak English, I said to myself as I approached him. He did. His English was almost perfect; he was polite and told me he would escort me to the British Consulate himself. He brought me to the building which housed the Consul, which was only about a ten–minute walk from where I had been standing for the whole, interminable afternoon. He rang the bell, bade me farewell and wished me good luck. What a gentleman, I thought to myself.

The door was promptly opened by a portly lady to whom I introduced myself, and before she could reply I quickly told her my story about posting a letter, losing my way and my ship sailing without me. She lapped it up and brought me inside to meet a secretary; I believe it was a secretary: she looked like a secretary.

She brought into a lounge, gave me a cup of coffee and told me to relax while she had a word with the boss. After about ten minutes an officer came and introduced himself. He said he was sorry to hear I had missed my ship, said 'you will of course stay the night here and we can arrange your passage home in the morning.' As easy as that: I could not believe my luck.

The next morning, a quick wash, breakfast and I would be on my way. The officer gave me two tickets, one for my passage to

England and the other for my passage home to Belfast. The officer drove me to the docks from where he told me the ship for England would be departing, which would be in a couple of hours' time. I thanked him for his kindness. He said it was all part of the job and wished me luck.

I arrived in Belfast two days later. Ironically, the ship which took me to Belfast was the Duke of Lancaster, a sister ship of the Duke of Rothesay.

My Ma was quite shocked to see me when I knocked her door at half eight in the morning. Drinking a big welcome mug of tea, and devouring a breakfast of fried soda farls and a couple of eggs, I started to tell Ma my story.

I exaggerated and tried not to lie, and said that I had gone ashore to look around Le Havre, lost my way and the ship had sailed without me. My Ma lapped it up; I was her favourite, so of course she would. Her only reservation was that they would miss me on the ship. I reassured her that they would not. After lunch I told Ma that I would go to see Beth and surprise her.

"I wouldn't bother, Kenny," my Ma quickly replied. This surprised me.

"What do you mean, Ma...?"

"From when you left, Beth has never visited the house again."

I repeated the question. My Ma went on to tell me that she had run into Beth about a week after I had left. Beth did not come up to the house anymore because she had met a new boy, and he must be her new boyfriend.

"But I've have only been away a few days! It didn't take her long to forget me..."

"There's plenty more fish in the sea, Kenny," my Ma reassured me. "You will soon meet plenty of other girls."

My Ma was not put out too much, but I bloody was. A few short days ago this pretty girl had sworn undying love. But forever did not last long. In my anger and first real experience of heartbreak, I promised that nobody would ever mess me about again. I put Beth out of my mind quicker than I thought I ever would, even though I had for a short while adored her to distraction.

91

Happiness is a matter of choice; and Beth had indeed made me very, very happy for the few short weeks I had known her. And I have never regretted anything that made me happy. Sailing the seas on a decent ship did just that.

In the next few days I would get myself sorted out. I wondered whether I would ever go to sea again. I did not know it then but in the next few months I would be on a ship once more.

The Sea and I were not done quite yet.

Chapter Twenty Four

Can't Wait

OCTOBER '59; BACK in Belfast. Sometimes it seemed like I never left this city for long, or worse still, was destined never to leave it. What was I going to do now? No ship, no job, no prospects.

The Inishowen Head had left me disenchanted with the Merchant Navy and I was really feeling sorry for myself now. Perhaps I should not have jumped ship; after all, the voyage was only for six or seven weeks. But that is a long time when you are lovesick and homesick.

My mother had explained to my sister's boyfriend Tommy all about the Inishowen Head sailing without me, and went on to tell him that I went ashore to post a letter, lost track of time and was left stranded in France.

I was relieved that my mother had mentioned it to Tommy as I would have been slightly embarrassed to tell him myself. Tommy gave me the impression that he thought no more about it; he was always diplomatic.

He said he would keep an eye open for me for any vacancy on a ship that came along, and asked me if I was still up for another ship. I quickly replied and reassured him that I certainly was.

October passed and then November without any opportunities coming my way. I had visited the shipping pool a few times but found nothing that would suit me there. I was beginning to feel down and began to wonder whether I should start looking for a job in civvy street in Belfast. But I knew in my heart that I did not want to live and work in Belfast, and my heart was telling me to travel. Then suddenly everything changed: once again, Tommy was coming to my rescue.

On the seventeenth of December Tommy called at our house and told me to put on my coat: we were going for a wee dander...

He started to tell me that a cargo ship called the La Primavera was due to dock in Belfast the following day, the eighteenth, and that there was a vacancy for a second cook and baker.

La Primavera

"Tommy, I can't bake!" I was quick to tell him.

"Never mind that, they are desperate to fill this vacancy and there's a good chance they will take you on."

Tommy reminded me that they could not sail without a second cook and baker, and I was in with a good chance with it being so close to Christmas as no one would want the bloody job.

Most people, sailors or not, and especially married men (or for that matter, single men), want to spend Christmas at home, understandably. Tommy and I went back and forth.

"Ken, I will get you on this ship."

"Tommy I really want this ship!"

"The job is yours, Ken, believe me, if you really want it."

"Tommy, I really want this ship!"

He went on to tell me that the La Primavera was only about a year old, spic–and–span and had a good captain on board, a real gentleman.

"Now if I get you this ship," Tommy told me, "be careful: watch what you are doing. Don't go posting letters in strange countries."

I knew at that moment that Tommy had suspected that I had jumped ship and that I had never gone near a post box to post a letter. But he was too much of a gentleman to reproach me about it.

"Tommy," I said, "I will never post another letter abroad."

On the nineteenth, Tommy and I went on board the La Primavera to meet the chef and the Chief Officer. We shook hands. The officer asked me jokingly was I a good cook; I replied, "But of course I am."

"Well, Mr. Patterson, the chef will take you to the galley," said the Chief Officer. "He will ask you a few questions. If he is satisfied, then I am satisfied. The ship sails at ten in the morning."

I took to the chef straight away. He was amiable, easy going and not in any way overbearing. I told him I was an assistant cook, but that I could not bake. He told me that there was no problem: he would do the baking on this trip, see to the cooking for the officers and that my job was to see to the rest of the crew.

"We will work together, muck in and help each other," he reassured me. "Are you happy with that, Ken?"

I certainly was happy with that.

"That will suit me fine, Chef."

"Too formal, Ken," he replied. "My name is Dave Smith."

Other than that, Dave asked what ship or ships I had sailed on before. And that was my interview.

"We sail at ten in the morning, Ken. I will give you a quick look at your cabin, let you get away to pack your stuff, and say your goodbyes."

Dave quickly showed me to where my cabin was; showed me inside and I was chuffed: it was big, with plenty of space. There was a built–in wardrobe and plenty of cupboards. This cabin was five star compared to my two other ships.

"Be here at eight thirty in the morning, Ken. I will have finished breakfast and will then give you a tour of the ship."

"I'll see you at eight thirty, Dave and thank you for your trouble."

"No problem," was his reply.

I was excited and on my way home I thanked my lucky stars. I was feeling well about the world. I knew that this ship was heading for America but that was about all. I was not really concerned and had a good feeling about this ship and about my future colleague, Dave Smith.

Indeed, I would be posting no more letters, although I would be visiting some exotic places.

Chapter Twenty Five

Mobile, Alabama

O N THE MORNING of the 20th December, 1959, I said my goodbyes. My mother was the only one in the house when I was about to leave; everyone had gone to work. I knew they would not take time off to see me off even when I had given them plenty of notice.

I grabbed my suitcase and said cheerio to my mother and that I would see her in a few weeks. The truth is I had no idea when I would see her again. Tommy had told me he would be there to see me off: what an absolute friend. He had turned out to be a very selfless man.

I walked up the gangplank of the La Primavera spot on eight thirty a.m., just as Dave Smith had requested. I went straight to the galley, about two yards from the gangplank, with my suitcase.

"Take your gear down to your cabin Ken, put your stuff away and I will give you a quick tour," Dave told me. "At ten a.m., if you didn't already know, we are setting sail for Mobile, Alabama, U.S.A."

I did not know! Through all the excitement and preparation

after landing this position, the thought had never entered my mind to enquire as to where we were going.

Nevertheless, the situation was completely different this time: there was no Beth continuously on my mind. That feeling had completely been erased from my brain. I was excited and truly looking forward to travelling to foreign lands. Travelling light, travelling far, far away from everyone and everything I knew.

I joined Dave in the galley and before he started to show me round the ship, he introduced me to a young lad called Jim Roberts, who turned out to be a galley boy like I had been.

He too had just joined the ship. Of course, that was another thing that had never entered my mind throughout all the excitement: I had moved up in the world. No galley deck to sweep and mop, no pots and pans to scrub. The only thing I would be doing with the pots and pans was cooking.

Every cargo ship carried a galley boy, or in civilian terms a kitchen porter. The only exception that I had come across was my last ship, The Inishowen Head, and I had had the misfortune of being a member of its crew, albeit thankfully for only a brief time. This was going to suit me fine.

We had two stewards on board and their duties included looking after the ships' officers: keeping their uniforms tidy, changing their bedding, serving their food, preparing and serving their drinks, and looking after the ship's laundry. They were kept quite busy.

We had a good little catering team: two cooks, two stewards and a galley boy. It turned out to be a small but happy team. Yes, there were five of us and out of the five, three were Jims: what are the odds on that?

There was Jim Roberts, the galley hand, and the two stewards were christened Jim Sloane and Jim Hanna. We had a few laughs out of that as did most of the crew. In order to keep things simple, Dave and I decided that the galley lad would be JR and the two stewards would be JS and JH. They were the B team; Dave and I were the A team.

Dave showed me around the ship quickly and reminded me once again that the ship would be departing come ten o' clock a.m. I did not need reminding: it was embedded in my mind. He told me to come to the galley at about eleven thirty to familiarise myself with the hobs, ovens, deep freeze and generally have a good look around and get a feel for it. I would help him prepare lunch. This suited me just right, and would give me a chance to watch the ship leaving and to see old Belfast: this would be the last time I would see her for quite a while.

I went up on deck about ten minutes before we were due to leave. At ten o' clock on the dot, the engines started roaring. Throw off the bow lines, let go the stern and we were moving. Sure enough, my sister's boyfriend Tommy and his old man were there to wave me off. The maritime influence is strong in Ulster. Belfast is a shipbuilding city and sea port. The coastline is long with many harbours.

It is a sight to see, sailing out of Belfast, and a sight I would not see again for a few months. This was the first time I would be taking a good look as we were departing Belfast, probably because this would be the last time I would see the city for quite a while. The different harbours, the river Lagan, the giant cranes, then the city and the landscape beyond, all slowly disappeared before my eyes.

I was going deep sea now and I would be interacting with people every day. If I had a problem with a crew member I would have no option but to work with him and keep the grudges aside; this to me seemed a sensible option. In the weeks to come perhaps one or two of the crew members should have stuck to that code.

I believe we sailed into Mobile harbour on or round about the twenty–ninth of December and, after loading and unloading, departed on the first of January 1960. Mobile was disappointing, simply because we never really got a chance to see the city. We didn't go ashore, as we were on a tight schedule, so all we really saw were the dockers and cargo being loaded and unloaded. The weather was bleak as was the harbour.

Christmas day had been uneventful: a few turkeys, a few drinks, a quiet day really, just like home in Belfast. In fact, the entire journey from Belfast to Alabama was uneventful. We had a rough sea for a couple of days but nothing too untoward the rest of the time. The ocean was quite benign and calm; most unusual, I thought, for that season of the year.

The crew members were getting to know each other; I was on nodding terms with most of them. I was enjoying my work in the galley and learning a few tricks from Dave. He taught me how to chop food quickly and skilfully without injuring my fingers...

We were cooking more or less the same food that I had cooked on my first ship; nothing too adventurous. Thankfully the members of the crew that I was cooking for were easily pleased; no complaints so far. There was nothing to complain about really: they were eating good quality well cooked dishes, even if I say so myself.

Dave revised the menus every day and from time to time had a good look at my efforts; he seemed satisfied. I was learning from Dave all the time, just as I had done with Tommy Burke on the Duke of Rothesay. Cooking is always a learning process.

I did know now that we would be heading for Los Angeles, San Francisco and then onto Asia; Japan, to be exact. I was on a different wavelength now and enjoying myself. Japan, I thought: that's a bloody long way away, something to really look forward to. A strange, faraway land with mysterious inhabitants that you read about when you were a youngster. My image of Japan was of fierce warriors, their hair tied up in a bun, and engaged in tribal wars. Of course the opposite was true, as I would discover.

On the afternoon of the twentieth of January we set sail for California, a trip of about two thousand three hundred miles. To get there, we had to cut through the Americas at their narrowest point.

The Panama Canal was fifty miles in length and one hundred and ten feet wide in the 1960s. You would think that this was sufficient room for all shipping, but with two-way traffic it was a tight fit for some modern container vessels and cruise ships; these giants require more space.

Today they are in the process of widening the canal – a huge undertaking in itself.

As soon as breakfast was finished I asked Dave if he would cut my hair; it was like a wet mop with the heat. I thought this was a bit cheeky on my part to ask Dave, but our chef did have a hairdressing set: scissors, combs and a hair clipper. He agreed, liking the idea of a guinea pig on which to try out his skills:

"How much do you want off, Ken?"

"I want the lot cut off."

This really pleased Dave as it took the pressure off him. Shearing me would require no skill or styling. So we brought a chair from the canteen out on deck, placed it in a bit of shade and soon an audience gathered for the show.

Dave proceeded with gusto, snapping away with the scissors, waving the comb around, and finally finishing off his performance with buzzing clippers. I was left completely bald and Sweeney Todd had even left me with a few abrasions. His skill as a chef was well known, but his skill as a hairdresser would be quickly forgotten.

When Dave had finished erasing my hair, there was soft applause from our small audience who, noticing that my bald head was garnished with a few small cuts, was in no hurry to invite the chef to cut their hair. At least Dave had performed his duty and I was grateful. It was wonderfully refreshing to be free of my shock of black hair in the tropical Panama heat.

Sweating in Central America, I was determined not to count the days, but to make the days count.

Chapter Twenty Six

California

FROM THE ATLANTIC Alabama to the Pacific California. On around the fifth day after leaving Mobile and going through Panama, we sailed under the iconic Golden Gate Bridge and into San Francisco Bay. We gawped from the deck at the bleak, forbidding and desolate Alcatraz penitentiary before heading into port.

Early that evening Jim Roberts and I took a cable car around the city; we also managed to walk up a couple of the steep, hilly streets.

We had a lovely couple of days in San Francisco, the city by the bay, where the iconic Tony Bennett had left his heart. I kept remembering my older brother Fred, back home in a faraway Belfast, who would sing this song for years in his local pub, but only whilst under the influence. Now I was here, walking the streets of that fantastic city and experiencing the vertigo of its dizzying charm.

Before we sailed we took on board two Swedish engineers who I was told would be inspecting and testing the ships' boilers and engines all the way to Japan. I found that probable as this was a comparatively young ship and the first significant inspection was due.

On the way to San Francisco, we had stopped briefly in Los Angeles. There we managed a quick trip ashore where we had a cup of coffee and then headed back.

Merchant Seaman Monument, San Francisco

After San Francisco, the next stop was Oakland: round the corner, so to speak. A quick cruise over the bay. We stopped in Oakland for the afternoon to refuel and pick up supplies; food mainly: fruit, bread, vegetables and meat, a few sides of beef and some lamb. In short, enough meat to fill our huge walk–in galley freezer.

All this was essential as our next stop would be Japan, a long way from Oakland: about eight thousand miles. As soon as everything was loaded on, we slipped our berth and were on our way to Japan.

This captain did not like to hang about.

The bread on board ship did not last too long. Apart from it losing its freshness, the crew devoured it as quickly as possible. Dave had been baking bread on our way to America and he would be baking a great deal more on our way to Asia. There was a large wooden cask in the galley about half the size of a beer barrel. Into this receptacle Dave would put his flour, yeast and water with a handful of salt, and would pound it with great ferocity, just like a boxer punching a heavy bag. It was bloody hard work, and I was thankful and relieved, very relieved in fact, with Dave's arrangement for me to feed the crew and for him to look after the officers and, most importantly for me, for him to bake the bread. The sweat would pour from him and some of it would end up in the dough. Dave would giggle at this and quipped that it would add a touch of flavour to the finished product. Whether it did or not was a matter of conjecture, but no one ever complained.

As I got to know Dave more as the days passed, I soon discovered that he was eccentric. He did not worry about anything and never panicked; I was convinced that our chef was quite mad, but a good kind of mad. Dave did not bother anyone and no one bothered him, and there was no reason to: he was very good at his job.

We sailed under the famous bridge once again and before long Alcatraz Prison appeared on the horizon. Alcatraz is located in the San Francisco bay area about one and a half miles from the city and is often referred to as 'The Rock'. And that is all it is. To me it was just a barren island with a grey, formidable, impenetrable penitentiary. Somewhere there inside, the likes of Al Capone had been incarcerated, as well as Robert Stroud, the "birdman" of Alcatraz made famous by the film starring Burt Lancaster.

Apparently there were a few attempts to escape from Alcatraz Prison involving over thirty inmates, and officially every attempt failed: the escapees were either killed or recaptured. Those who did escape either disappeared without a trace or were perhaps killed by the ocean and the elements. But the lack of any corpses gave rise to the theory that some attempts were successful.

From the safety and comfort of the deck, and as we sailed by, I tried to imagine the attempt. As soon as you entered the water, which I presume would have been a little on the cold side, there were quite a few different species of sharks swimming in the bay; Great Whites were frequent visitors. Soon, however, there would be no need for any more escape attempts: in 1963, a few years after I set eyes upon it, Alcatraz was closed by order of Robert Kennedy. It had only been in operation for 29 years, but entered the imagination of the United States and far beyond.

The ship passed by that miserable, wretched hulk of rock quickly, and we were on our way to Asia. I did not know it then, but I would be back in California again in a few weeks' time.

I was now a long way from Belfast, but this was not the Inishowen Head: this was a lovely ship with lovely living quarters, decent colleagues and most importantly, I was not feeling any pangs of homesickness.

So far everything was fine. So far I was enjoying myself. So far.

Chapter Twenty Seven

Sharks and Whales

ABOUT TWO–AND–a–half thousand miles from Oakland, California, and in the North Pacific, we spotted the Hawaiian Islands. A beautiful sight: golden, sandy beaches with palm trees cascading down to an inviting sky blue sea. How I wished the ship would put into port there.

Then out of the blue another beautiful sight: two humpback whales had decided to keep us company for a while. These massive but graceful animals were swimming alongside the ship.

The captain had already messaged the engine to reduce speed to enable the crew to get a good look at these magnificent beasts. They were in our company for quite a few minutes until they decided that they had had enough of showing us their aquatic skills. They then sped off in a different direction to a round of applause from the crew. Those two beauties had made my day. I was enthralled. This was why I had gone deep sea.

Just then a gigantic rainbow appeared in the sky, and no sooner had its arch formed than the heavens opened and a torrent of rain came falling down. I was quite surprised to see this deluge of rain: in my naivety I had believed it could not rain in this paradise of islands. But it did, and bloody hard at that. I scuttled back to the Galley. The ship picked up speed and set herself on a course for Japan.

Everything was fine on board ship. The crew was well fed and watered. On a morning or two each week, if they desired, they could have a full English breakfast. If they chose cereals, then there was plenty of choice. For lunch there was usually a bowl of soup and a sandwich or two. Dinner invariably consisted of lasagne, stew, cottage pie, shepherd's pie, steaks, lamb and pork chops, etc. Those staff members who were off duty could have a beer or two to wash it down. A well–fed crew is a happy one.

Adjacent to the galley was the crew's small canteen. There was a hatch on the wall of the canteen which lengthened out and I would often put their food there and the crew would help themselves. Sometimes, if I had the inclination, I would bring it to their tables, but most of the time the crew members liked to help themselves. This method seemed advantageous for them, especially when they were on duty and their time limited.

Perhaps it was me and probably because I was in close proximity to them on a regular basis, I seemed to detect a tension amongst two or three of the crew members, a raised voice here and there and some unanswered question. Those particular guys were from Belfast. The remainder of the crew were mainly Northern Irish, a handful from Southern Ireland, a couple of Scousers, and Dave Smith my colleague was from London. He said he was born beside Bow Bells and was therefore a true cockney. I did not believe him: he did not have a so–called cockney accent.

Two of the able seamen came to the galley one evening when we had finished dinner and asked Dave if he could have any blood from a carcass in the freezer, and any kidneys, liver or any old bits of leftover stale meat and bones.

"What's your game?" Dave asked them. "Are you not getting enough food? You want to scavenge for leftovers?"

The two deck hands bent over double laughing at this retort. They started to explain to Dave that the ship would be anchoring in a couple of days in the middle of the Pacific Ocean. Engines would be stopped for the sole purpose of the two Swedish engineers on board conducting a survey of the engine room. When the ship came to a stop, they were going to do a spot of fishing down at the aft end of the ship. Dave said that he would see what he could muster.

These two deckhands shouted into the galley for Dave's attention, and as he consented, he told them to step into the galley. Dave was an easy going guy; with most things he could not care, but as far as the galley was concerned, that was his territory, his kingdom. Dave's attitude was quite simple: food was prepared and cooked in this vicinity, and chiefly because of hygiene concerns no one entered this hallowed ground without the chef's permission. This rule also extended in its application to the officers.

Two days later, as the deckhands had mentioned, the ship came gradually to a stop in the middle of the Pacific Ocean. This would enable the Swedish engineers with the assistance of the ships' engineers to carry out a robust inspection of the young engines to see if they were performing one hundred percent as they should be.

It was about seven o'clock in the evening as I made my way to the after end of the ship, along with most of the crew, to witness what these two seamen were getting up to.

Not a ripple on the water: it was like a sheet of glass. On board, complete quiet; absolute silence. A full moon.

These two lads prepared to drop a mixture of meat fat, kidneys, rotten food and a bucket of blood into the water. I had gathered by now that this was a shark expedition. Ten minutes went by; not a single ripple broke the placid surface of the vast ocean around us. Twenty minutes. Still nothing. Half an hour passed. I was about to retire to my cabin disappointed by all this fuss for nothing when I was sure that I saw a couple of fins about fifteen feet out. Can't be, I thought to myself as I rubbed my eyes. About three seconds later two unmistakable shadows emerged from the gloom: two massive snouts full of terrifying teeth.

The First Officer, who considered himself a peerless authority on the subject of fish, informed anyone within ear shot that these two creatures were indeed Grey Reef Sharks.

Grey Reef Sharks or not, my heart was drumming at the sight of these fearsome animals. They span back and forth, inspecting the waste food, then after a couple of approaches and as suddenly as they had appeared, they slipped back into the darkness of the Pacific Ocean.

I was awed and impressed by their grace and power, and of course their inquisitiveness.

I retired to my bed that night with a cup of cocoa, and went to sleep with a picture of these magnificent creatures in my head. I have never forgotten them. We had witnessed these Grey Reef Sharks swimming in the calm, placid and seemingly peaceful Pacific.

Within a few days, and off the coast of Japan, this ocean would change dramatically from tranquil to frightening, and be accompanied in its malice by life–threatening gale force storms.

Chapter Twenty Eight

Stormy Welcome

MARCH '60; THIRTY miles off the coast of Japan. The calm sea that we had enjoyed when we were watching those two sleek Grey Reef Sharks sniff at the food we had left for them, and sniff at it again without ever bloody touching it and then slink off into the depths of the Pacific, was about to disappear.

Sleet was raining down on us, followed by sheets of snow. There was a roar of thunder followed by sheets of lightning and the wind was picking up with gusto. Within a matter of minutes the ship was beginning to rock and roll. The waves were growing in height, lashing the ship and spilling onto the decks; all this, in a very short space of time.

A message came over the tannoy from the bridge, warning the ship's crew to batten down the hatches. Secure everything that can be secured.

It was about five thirty in the evening. Dave and I immediately cleared everything off the hob, and took a pan of rice out of the oven. We didn't think anyone would be partaking of dinner this evening and of course we were right. Dave said he was going to his cabin. I told him that I was going to have a quick cigarette on deck just outside the galley and then retire to my cabin: to relative safety. He advised me not to hang about. Jim Roberts had already disappeared.

As I was enjoying my cigarette an almighty wave pounded the bulkhead and landed me on my ass. I lifted myself up and stepped into the galley. Why I did not hasten to my cabin is beyond me. Habit, I guess, and also the fact that my cabin was further away than the galley. Nevertheless, after that huge wave all I wanted in the world was to get inside as soon as possible.

There was a permanent potato machine concreted into the deck of the galley. It stood four feet tall and had a considerable girth. This was a labour–saving device: a bucket of potatoes would be poured into the machine and this wonderful contraption would wash and peel the spuds. But on this particular evening I would be putting it to a different use.

The ship was bobbing like a cork and I could not stop myself from being thrown all over the galley. I was thankful that this potato machine was where it was, and lucky enough to put my arms around it and hang on for dear life. Together we danced a strange and desperate tango, and I was immensely relieved that there were no witnesses to our performance.

I had never before seen a storm with such terrifying power; violent, hurricane-force winds spurring on gigantic waves. The wind direction had changed and they were now hitting the bow of the ship. I could hear them overhead and I was aft off the ship. They were covering the length of this vessel.

I was later told that the captain could have avoided this storm by making a detour, but he would not. As far as he was concerned the company was time and time was money. He was therefore determined to meet this storm head on and go through it. There was no way that he was going to miss his allocated berthing spot if he had anything to do with it.

Otaru, where we were heading, was a harbour town with a busy port and many ships bound for Japan docked there. If he missed this berth he would probably have to wait for hours before another one was available. He had a valuable cargo to unload and there was no way this would be jeopardised because of a 'windy sea'. A windy sea: I thought afterwards that we almost lost the ship. That old seafarer had experienced many rough seas. It was port or bust for him, the committed company man, and the crew came a firm second.

I had had my arms clung tightly round this spud machine, the first figure I had caressed since Beth in Belfast, and dared not move freely while the storm was raging. If you were not holding on to something you could sustain serious injury.

About an hour after the storm had begun the worst was over. I left the safety of my gargantuan paramour, the potato machine, and made my way on deck. I had to have a cigarette. As I lit my fag, I could see the coastline of Japan in the distance. We had made it through. The relief seeped through my body. I noticed my hand trembling as I drew upon the cigarette and sucked in nicotine courage.

After a storm of unprecedented ferocity the ship and I limped our way into port. We berthed in Otaru. The dockers started to unload the cargo. I made my way to my cabin and had a cup of cocoa.

This had been an experience I did not wish to repeat in the near future, or any future for that matter. I looked in on Dave and our galley boy Jim; they were still alive. Dave had seen it all before. Jim, like I, had not, and he was still shaking. But he had made it through to see another day. Dave mentioned that he suspected that not many crew would turn up for breakfast and it turned out that he was right. A scary storm did offer one advantage: it meant less work on the morning shift.

When the sea is in a rage it is best left alone. I had been reminded once again, and in dramatic fashion, that the sea is a master whom we disrespect or ignore at our peril.

Chapter Twenty Nine

R&R in Otaru

AFTER THAT TERRIFYING ordeal the night before, six of the crew managed to show their faces for breakfast. There was no food on the hob and all they could manage was a bowl of cereal and a few mugs of hot tea. That was an easy morning for our small team of catering staff.

The three amigos in our team, Jim Sloane, Jim Hanna and our galley boy, Jim Roberts, were discussing whether or not we would be going ashore that evening to sample the night life of Otaru, if in fact there was a night life.

Dave Smith joined our group and said there were a few crew members venturing abroad onto terra firma. He went on to say that these guys had visited Japan on a few occasions and certainly knew their way around. He told us that if we were interested we could wait at the gangplank for them around seven thirty.

The three Jims and I agreed simultaneously that was a brilliant arrangement. I, like everyone else, had not seen solid ground for quite a while, so it was great to get out of my cooks' whites and into fresh, clean clothes. We were not disappointed and I could not believe my eyes when about ten crew approached us.

"Let's go, lads!"

When I set foot that evening on Japanese soil for the first time, it was like stepping back in time. The architecture was something that I had not seen the likes of before. I had seen pictures of it in books, but in real life it was completely strange and seemingly foreboding to one who had been lost in Le Havre.

The streets that we started to walk down were really narrow and the snow was up to our ankles. Snow stretched three or four feet up the walls of the tiny buildings in these narrow streets, as if a giant had effortlessly heaped it there. Everything was quiet and atmospheric. I was out of my depth here. Jim Roberts was out of his depth here. We were the youngest crew members on the ship. Yes, alright, we had been round the south and west coasts of America, but at least they spoke the same language and the culture was more or less the same. This country was another planet to us.

It was not long before we reached our first port of call. JR and I followed the crew into our first inn: a dark, dirty little hovel. Everyone seemed to be drinking shorts, so Jim and I had a couple of cheap whiskies; then on to another little tavern, much the same as the first, and another couple of cheap whiskies.

All this was in the space of about thirty minutes. These deckhands were not hanging about. It was as if they were on a mission to get somewhere in particular and were just warming up for the big event.

There was no way Jim and I were going to lose them so we struggled to keep up with them, knocking back the spirits one after the other. We had no desire or plans to be on our own in this strange country called Japan.

The big event came along at the next inn we entered. It was on a main thoroughfare and it was a different set up completely. It was large and spacious, and one of the first things I noticed was that there were a lot of small booths, private sitting areas discreetly placed against the walls all the way round the interior. The second thing I noticed was that a lot of women were swarming towards us.

In my innocence, I thought that they were customers like us and delighted to see foreigners in their local inn. I discovered later they were not.

There was an officer cadet from the ship in our party. This young man was six foot two inches of well–muscled body and was extraordinarily handsome in a way that would have made Cary Grant look ugly.

Within seconds of us entering the inn, a dozen or so women surrounded him and for the time being ignored everyone else. They swarmed around the bemused cadet. I could tell the other crew members were unhappy and jealous, and wishing they had this guy's good looks if only for tonight. As it slowly dawned on me what was happening, Jim Sloane realised I was slightly confused, bewildered even, and informed me that these females were escort girls.

Escort girls my ass: I was not that backward.

After a few moments, when things settled down, Jim Sloane and I were ushered over to one of these booths by two women who looked like they were about thirty years old. We sat down. Jim was laughing. I was still bewildered, but I thought to myself what pleasant, friendly ladies these were. They introduced themselves as Sue and Kim. Obviously they had adopted these Western names for convenience. So–called Sue called the hovering waitress over softly and, without asking us what we would like to drink, ordered four gin and tonics. Jim paid for these and Sue handed him a ticket. There was not much conversation beyond asking us what ship Johnny was from, what country Johnny was from, and if Johnny liked Japan. Jim Sloane and I were both called Johnny for the evening.

The serving of drinks went on for about three hours, and we were given tickets after each round. Jim was paying for these drinks and told me not to worry, I could square up with him when we get back to the ship.

After what I think was twelve tickets and twelve gins, Jim was stone sober and I was in an inebriated state. I attribute my youthful innocence about such matters to my Presbyterian upbringing.

The two women beckoned us to go with them to their house for a drink. Jim was definitely up for that. I did not have much of a choice as everybody had gone their own ways, and Jim was not

115

going to leave me on my own. I realised that Jim Sloane was one of the crew who had been here before and was an old hand at this game.

A taxi ride later through long, narrow streets, and we arrived at this pretty little house. After everyone had taken their shoes off, we were ushered into a sort of lounge. Adjacent to that were what looked like two bedrooms.

I remember some of the story of what happened next.

We had a couple more gins; these people certainly liked their gin and tonics. But as Jim told me the next day, Johnny and Johnny were drinking alcohol whereas the women were drinking tonics.

Still in a state of drunkenness, I recall these two women taking their clothes off and washing themselves in a sunken bath and inviting us to watch them. I was wobbly now and could not believe what I was seeing.

"Fuck this," I said to Jim, "I'm off!"

Jim grabbed me before I fell and put me on a mattress on the floor. As I found out later, this is the Japanese bed: a mattress on the floor. As soon as Jim had placed me on the mattress, I fell unconscious.

I awoke the next morning, as fresh as a daisy. Jim was already dressed and began to tell me about the lovely time he had enjoyed with these two women. Johnny minus Johnny had enjoyed the favours of not one woman, but two. Johnny, Sue and Kim.

When I was dressed, an old lady dressed in a kimono entered the room with a tray and began to pour us a cup of black, tasteless tea: all part of the service, I supposed. She introduced herself as Mama–San. Jim told me that that was the Japanese term for 'mother'.

What friendly people, I thought to myself: Jim up to no good with her daughters and then their mother serving us tea. We felt at ease in this house, although it was awkward for Jim and me sitting cross legged on the floor. Afterwards, and after Jim had parted with some yen, we were put in a taxi and arrived at our ship in time for breakfast.

Over the years I have thought a great deal about that strange night, and I have never been able to figure out or recall what exactly happened. Perhaps this is just as well.

Although no harm came to me, I vowed from that moment on that never again in my life would I get drunk in a strange drinking establishment, in a foreign town or city, unless of course I was surrounded by my friends.

Chapter Thirty

Karaoke

LATE SPRING '60. About 800 miles and two days from Otaru, we were entering Yokohama, the second largest city in Japan and the country's largest port. Yokohama was the first harbour city introduced to the world as the entrance to Japan. This city looked large and grand: a bustling port and as far as I could see a busy, vigorous city.

Otaru, which we had visited a couple of days before, seemed medieval; Yokohama, in contrast, looked modern. This was the beginning of the sixties. Elvis Presley's photo was appearing everywhere on billboards. The cinemas were still running *King Creole* and *Love Me Tender*, even though these films had first started showing in the late fifties in America. Japan was just beginning to wake up to this new craze.

It was five o' clock in the evening when we tied up in Yokohama port. Dave Smith had told the ship's crew we would be having an early dinner: this would enable everyone who was not on duty to visit the town and sample its night life.

There was no shortage of volunteers for this expedition and the three Jims and I were looking forward to it after our adventures in Otaru a few days before. Dave Smith, Jim Roberts, Jim Sloane, Jim Hanna and I met up again at seven thirty, more or less with the same crew that we had been with from our last outing on mainland Japan.

We passed a couple of hostelries before we entered a huge bar; well, it actually looked like a club, and was fancy in appearance. Music was playing as we walked in. I did not realise as I entered that club that I was in for quite a shocking, surprising and educational night. No girls approached us as they did in Otaru when we walked towards the bar. Blimey, I thought, this was sophisticated. Elvis was singing *King Creole*. Were my eyes and ears deceiving me? This was incredible, this noise coming from a huge machine set on a stage, with a huge well-fed cat guarding it. We were told to sit down and a waitress would take our orders.

After Elvis was finished, a Japanese youth jumped up with a microphone in his hand and started trying to emulate the King whilst the music to *King Creole* was playing. This was the first time that I and the others had seen or heard anything like this. Pretty nifty, I thought.

The Japanese youth did not do a bad job, if you forget the accent. I was to learn that evening that this was called Karaoke, a new phenomenon to hit Japan. Of course, I had never before heard this word describing that Japanese invention which was still in its early days.

Karaoke originated in Japan. 'Kara' comes from 'karappo', meaning empty; and 'oke' is shortened from 'okesutura', meaning orchestra. Karaoke therefore means 'empty orchestra'.

As I was to learn that night, it was more than a matter of simple leisure: Karaoke was becoming an activity fully embedded in the intricate Japanese work culture, being a typical way to relax for Japanese businessmen. It was taken very seriously and its practitioners put great effort into entertaining their audience. It was quite demanding and you had to work the crowd.

I learnt that you can go into a bar in Japan and not drink alcohol, but refusing to sing was a definite mistake. Japanese people do not let you off the hook, and that lesson was about to be learned by Jim Sloane.

After the Japanese youth had sang *King Creole* to a round of applause, a little man in a smart suit approached our table and went straight to Jim Sloane.

"You sing!" he commanded. Jim of course was struck dumb and looked flabbergasted.

"No thank you," Jim managed to utter eventually.

A bad mistake: the Japanese fella was joined by another who was also dressed immaculately in a smart suit. These two Japanese bankers immediately separated Jim Sloane from his comfortable seat and his gin and tonic, placed him on the stage and thrust a microphone into his shaking hands. The rest of us did not know whether to laugh or cry.

In the meantime, while this drama with Jim Sloane was being played out, Dave Smith brought it to my attention that Jim Hanna was sat across the room with a lovely young Japanese girl and an old withered man who we were to learn was her papa. The crafty bugger had wasted no time in introducing himself.

As Dave and I were watching this trio with great interest, the old man got up, bowed to Jim, shook hands with him and excused himself.

"That lucky bastard has struck gold this time, Ken," Dave said to me.

"He didn't hang about," I replied.

Poor Jim Sloane was now on the stage and probably wishing he was where Jim Hanna was. I realised that night how aggressive the Karaoke tribe can be. I wondered what was going through Jim's mind. What if the crowd did not like his rendition? What if things were thrown at him because of his lacklustre warbling? Jim was lost up there, shaking like a leaf.

"What like to sing?" his captors asked him.

"Love Me Tender," came out of Jim's mouth, probably before he had realised it.

"Good! We put the music on." Jim's kidnappers were beaming with delight.

The music started playing and Jim started singing. It was awful; the audience remained silent and dazed. The bar cat was sat just out of reach of me; had it been a bit closer I would have chucked it at Jim. We endured the racket for about three minutes before finally, mercifully, Jim stumbled off the stage, not to applause but moans and groans and complete derision. Jim had truly ruined a great song.

We all decided it was time to leave before the cheeky bastards decided to pick on one of us for the next act, but after Jim Sloane the crowd needed a few minutes to recover. That gave us precious time to make our escape.

Before we took our leave I hastened to the table where my friend Jim Hanna was sitting with his pretty young thing. He introduced me to her.

"Ken, this is Akiri. Akiri, this is my friend, Ken."

"So pleased to meet you, Ken–san."

Her English was pretty good, which was just as well, because Jim's Japanese was non– existent.

"Are you coming, Jim?" I asked him. "We're leaving now."

"I'm staying a while longer, Ken. I'll get a taxi back to the ship."

I looked at beautiful Akiri and could understand without any doubts why Jim was in no hurry to leave this lovely creature. But I wanted to get back to the ship. The night had been quite an experience, an eventful eye opener for this young man called Ken from Crumlin.

Jim and I said our farewells.

Chapter Thirty One

Sayonara

DEEP IN SLEEP in my cosy little cabin. A loud banging on my door. A rude awakening at one o' clock in the bloody morning. Before I could rub my eyes and shout out for them to stop, Jim Hanna pushes open my door.

"Why don't you come in, Jim; please don't stand on ceremony."

"I'm sorry Ken for the noise and waking you," Jim blurted out. "I've just arrived back. Akiri arranged a taxi for me back to the ship."

"Lovely girl, Jim," I said.

"Ken, I'm in love," Jim confessed. "I can't get her out of my thoughts."

"Give it time," I said sarcastically, still fuming at the early wake–up call. "You've only just met her."

"But it seems I've known her all my life."

I had heard that saying before quite a few times in the Lyceum Picture House, but never in real life. Jim was now on his second cigarette.

"I'm pleased for you, old mate, and I hope things go well

122

for you," I told him. "But how can they? You'll be seeing your girlfriend tonight, but tomorrow morning we'll be sailing for America."

"I'm well aware of that, Ken. I'll be seeing Akiri tonight at her home. I'm going to meet her parents formally. I've already met her father; he's a nice person."

"Once again, I hope everything goes well for you tonight, Jim, But what are your plans after that, assuming that everything goes well?"

"We've pledged our love for each other," Jim said. "We've bonded." How could I argue with that? "We'll write to each other every day till we meet again, which will be as soon as possible as far as we're both concerned." Again, how could I argue with that? True love or true infatuation. Either way, Jim was smitten. "Akiri has expressed to me a longing to come to Britain," Jim went on. "Ireland, specifically. Well of course, as I come from there."

"But what about her parents?" says I. "Will they be keen on her leaving Japan?"

"That's what we'll be discussing tonight, along with a host of other things," Jim said. "I have a feeling, having met her father, that he is open to the idea. As far as her doting father is concerned, what his daughter wants she will get…"

"I most sincerely for your sake hope so, Jim."

I thought to myself that convincing the mother would be a different prospect altogether.

After about an hour Jim left me and returned to his cabin, whistling and waking everyone up. Within seconds I went straight back to sleep. I was delighted for Jim but sleep was more important to me at that particular moment than his romantic bliss.

Everything went back to normal on board after the strange night before. Jim was full of it, himself and the world, annoying everyone with his non–stop whistling and singing, but he did sound much better than his workmate Jim Sloane. A wailing cat sounded better than Jim Sloane's rendition of an Elvis classic. Young Jim was certainly bitten, deeply in love, or whatever that feeling is.

That evening after dinner was finished I retreated to my cabin, sat down and opened a tin of beer. Putting the can to my mouth for my first sip, I heard a knock at the door. A gentle knock.

"Come in…" Jim Hanna opens my cabin door and comes in.

"That's a quiet entrance, Jim," I said. "Not like the early hours of this morning when you nearly took the door off its hinges."

"I know, Ken," said Jim. "I apologise again for the early wake–up call, but I was really excited, my heart was thumping, and I had to get it all out."

"And I was the unlucky one you picked on, Jim."

"Jim Sloane is a good workmate, Ken, and a good friend, but I consider you my best friend, so I thought it only fitting I tell you. I had to tell someone. I knew you would keep it to yourself."

Jim went on to tell me that if he had told Jim Sloane then by now it would be all ever the ship, and for obvious reasons that was the last thing he wanted to occur.

"I really don't want anyone to know of my plans, Ken," Jim told me. What were his plans? Something perhaps he was hiding from me. "I'm off now Ken, wish me luck."

"Remember Jim, we are leaving Yokohama, Japan, in the morning after breakfast." I emphasised the word 'Japan'.

"I am well aware of that, mate."

I wished Jim all the best, and hoped he would get on well with Akiri's parents, especially the important one: the mother–san.

We shook hands firmly. I once again wished my mate well. "I will see you later and you can tell me everything."

Jim did not say, "I will see you later" or "I will see you in the morning." Jim said "thank you, Ken" and "goodbye!"

I wondered about that and felt uneasy, but I just couldn't put my finger on what was strange about the whole affair. Jim was doing all this in haste and that certainly alarmed me. In the end, those were the last words that my mate Jim Hanna ever spoke to me.

The next morning with breakfast cooked, coffee and tea brewed, only one steward, Jim Sloane, turned up for duty. Where was Jim Hanna? Dave Smith asked me if I had any idea. I told him I had none. He went down to Jim's cabin, and after ten minutes told us that there was no Jim. He went on to say that his cabin was tidy, the bunk was made but some of his clothes had gone.

After this, rumours started circulating. Did he run into trouble? Did he lose his way back to the ship? Was he drunk and sleeping it off somewhere? All these rumours were pie in the sky. Jim knew how to handle himself: he would never become inebriated or put himself in a position which he could not get out off.

After breakfast, Dave Smith and I had a thorough search of Jim's cabin and, sure enough, Jim had left a sealed envelope in his bottom drawer. Jim had addressed the envelope to the captain. Dave gave it to one of the ships' officers who gave it to the captain.

After half an hour the same officer told us that the note had briefly said, ironically, "Goodbye Captain, goodbye chaps. Sorry Captain, but I will not be coming to America with you."

I walked away, went to my cabin and had a really good laugh.

We were due to depart at nine o'clock, but the captain - and I thought it was very good of him, given how obsessed he was by schedule - delayed the departure for a couple of hours, "just in case the lad changes his mind," were his words.

At eleven o' clock that morning the ship departed Yokohama, without Jim. I was not sad: I had an overwhelming feeling that Jim would be alright in spite of my many misgivings. After all, Jim Hanna was from Belfast and Japan was a million miles away. Our cultures were completely different. The language was completely alien to us. Jim could not speak a word of Japanese but I suppose if everything went well, and I emphasise if everything went well, Jim was smart enough to learn the basics of the language. Besides, Akiri was familiar with the English language, a skill which could overcome many hurdles.

Jim was a huge Marlon Brando fan; he told me that he had seen the film Sayonara many times. In the 1957 film, Marlon Brando plays Ace Gruver, an American military officer who falls in love with a theatre entertainer named Hana–ogi. His friend, Joe Kelly, also falls in love with a Japanese girl whom he marries, which leads to their experiencing prejudice from the US military. When he is ordered back to the US, Joe realises that he will not be able to take his pregnant wife with him, and they commit suicide together to prevent separation. This spurs on Gruver to marry Hana-ogi in spite of the problems they will encounter. When asked by a reporter what he will say to both his military superiors and the Japanese who will not take kindly to the marriage, Gruver replies, "Tell 'em we said *Sayonara.*" I often wondered later on whether this film influenced Jim's decision to jump ship.

I would miss Jim as would all of his friends, but he had a lot going for him. For the brief time that I had seen him and Akiri together, they seemed to me to be at one with each other. He was six-feet tall and a good looking Irish lad. She was five-feet tall and a good looking Japanese girl. What could go wrong?

Not every flower comes to bloom but I had a feeling that this romance would do just that. I only wished that I had had the opportunity to say one last word to Jim...

Sayonara.

Chapter Thirty Two

Queensbury Rules

IT WOULD HAVE pleased me to stay a few more days in Yokohama: to my young eyes this city seemed well ahead of its time. Japan impressed me greatly: its courteous people, its refined culture. Not least of all its diversity, from medieval Otaru to ultra-modern Yokohama.

Over the years I have often reminisced about this beautiful country and felt the desire to return one day.

It was just after midday and we had left Japan behind us. A school of dolphins, which had been escorting us, disappeared into the distance as suddenly as they had appeared alongside our ship. At this time my thoughts turned to my mate Jim Hanna and his absence: he would be missed.

We were sailing the Pacific Ocean towards America. After that, on to the Atlantic Ocean via the Panama Canal. Apart from the absence of Jim Hanna, everyone and everything was back to normal and shipshape. Jim Sloane of course would be missing his friend and workmate, not least of all because of the heavier workload that now befell him. Jim Sloane was assured by the captain that a replacement for Jim Hanna would be waiting to join the ship when it docked in America; when it docked in Portland, Oregon, to be exact. Portland would be the first port of call; until then, everyone would chip in to help Jim Sloane.

Jim Roberts, the galley boy, would be the one that would assist Jim Sloane more than anyone else. When he had a few minutes to spare, he would don a crisp white steward's jacket and manage a spot of serving in the officers' restaurant. Jim adapted to this quite well, just like a natural. Dave did the baking and I did most of the cooking as we first agreed, although Dave would help to cook for the officers.

Their dishes were sometimes more sophisticated than the rest of the crew, but only occasionally: they were just tarted up a little. Keep them happy, Ken, and we will not see them for most of the voyage, Dave assured me. Their dishes were not much different from the rest of the crew; they were just tarted up a little.

"If it looks good, Ken," Dave would say, "they'll think it's good and eat it."

This was Dave's simple, culinary philosophy. Yes, things were going well; everything was running normally. No one had defected or jumped ship that I knew off. Dave was thumping the dough again to make bread and on occasion would bake a batch of apple tarts and a few little individual fancy pastries. This crew was being well and truly pampered. What could possibly go wrong?

A few weeks back I had imagined there was a slight atmosphere among some members of the crew. I dismissed this notion at the time. But now, on leaving Japan, I sensed it again. I sensed tension.

I would cook for the rest of the crew and serve them the food in their canteen which was adjacent to the galley. I was in a position to notice anything untoward. There was adequate seating in the canteen and plenty of space. But I began to notice how crew members, who used to sit in relatively close proximity and chat incessantly as they ate, were now beginning to sit apart. This would not mean anything to a newcomer on board ship, but I was feeding these guys three times a day. I gradually noticed the subtle changes. Where there had been chit chat, now there was almost complete silence.

Something was not right, but I could not put my finger on what was the reason. I mentioned this to Dave who dismissed my suspicions immediately, and told me that I had a runaway imagination. Perhaps, although I had noticed that bubbly conversations had disappeared. Something was not quite right and the thought nibbled and gnawed away at my mind little by little.

After dinner one evening, around seven o' clock and about three days away from Japan, I lit a cigarette and started my daily walk around the deck. It was a warm night, a quiet sea, and everything was calm and peaceful. Suddenly that peace and calm was broken: I heard a commotion, looked ahead about fifteen feet and saw two guys locked in combat. I could not believe my eyes. I saw how these two were trying to grab each other's legs to try to heave the other over the ship's side into the Pacific Ocean below - to commit murder.

This seemed unreal. I actually rubbed my eyes. I thought I was seeing things, but I soon realised that I was not.

I rushed to Dave Smith's cabin and told him what I had just witnessed. This time he believed me. I told him that they were two deck crew, so he alerted the Bosun who was their immediate boss, who quickly alerted an officer.

They ran to the commotion, the fight, only this time the two deckhands had been joined by another four deckhands who were also having a go. These guys were really at it: punching, kicking, head–butting and scratching.

The Bosun and two officers were quickly able to control the situation. The men were quickly escorted back to their quarters and would appear before the captain the next day. I heard from Dave that they were severely reprimanded and cautioned.

I could not believe that this had taken place on a British ship on the high seas. But stranger things throughout history have happened on British ships on the high seas. Dave did mention that these six combatants were three Catholics and three Protestants; it probably meant nothing to Dave but as far as I was concerned it was significant and frightening, and brought back bad memories.

I would not forget that night in a hurry, although it did not bother Dave: nothing bothered Dave.

The next day of course was different from our usual routine: everyone by this time had heard about the fighting the night before. Nothing stays secret on a ship for long. Hardly anyone turned up for breakfast. At lunchtime it was almost empty in the crew's canteen. Some of the crew would take their food back to their cabin. The rot had set in: things had changed, routine was broken and I was afraid. This could happen again; the tension was becoming unbearable...

Three Protestants, three Catholics, Northern Irish, bad feeling, a restricted space and a very frightened lad from Crumlin who wanted nothing of it.

This was a ship full of Catholics and Protestants in the midst of the Pacific Ocean. We would soon be going through the Panama Canal and then we would be in the midst of the Atlantic Ocean. This could be the start of more fights. Religious sectarianism was rearing its ugly head, even on the other side of the world. It had started and as far as I was concerned, despite the captain's reprimand, this would happen again.

I had been on this ship a few months now and this latest episode had me thinking of Belfast. That disease I called homesickness was looming in my thoughts once more. I blamed the fighting for my relapse.

A few more days and we would arrive in America. Let us hope peace would return, I thought, at least until Portland and terra firma.

Chapter Thirty Three

Enough

JAPAN TO PORTLAND, Oregon, was a distance of almost five thousand miles and about two weeks for a ship in the 1960s. The captain had admonished the trouble makers. That was that. His job was to meet deadlines, adhere to schedule as much as possible, unload cargo, take on cargo and get us and the cargo to the ship's destination safely. After all, he had officers under his command and to them he delegated. They would keep a safe ship, a happy ship and, on the whole, in the next few days things were as normal as they could be. But I believed that peace would not resume.

Dirty looks and sarcastic remarks: that would be the pattern from now on.

I noticed a hell of a difference: Protestants and Catholics, with a few exceptions, were more or less sticking to their own kind as much as possible while off duty. This I did not like. Before, everyone had more or less mixed together in each other's company. Now, no. It was ominous and I was sad, wary and nervous. I knew things would not be the same again, but I was hoping there would be no more fights. In that aspect alone I was being optimistic and hopeful. I knew that the next time there was a confrontation, which could lead to a fight or worse, then it would take place out of sight.

When dinner was finished, I went for my usual dander. Before the fighting had started, most of the time I was the only person who took an evening walk. Now I noticed a couple of crew talking and a few steps on another three chatting. That would not be out of the ordinary, but the strange thing is that I knew these guys and they did not acknowledge my presence.

Something was brewing, but perhaps I was imagining all this. I retired to my cabin and decided that an evening excursion was out of the question, at least for the time being.

The ship had remained incident free by the time we made our way into a sunny Portland in the morning. Portland is a town at the northern end of Tillamook Bay, gateway to the magnificent Pacific Ocean.

After dinner that night, most of the crew had finished their meal when it all started again. Whereas before the previous altercation had involved only deck crew, on this occasion a handful of donkey men and firemen from the engine room crew were at it too. One guy had started pushing another guy, and they started shouting at each other. At that point I started shouting too, but for Dave.

"What's up, Ken?" Dave shouted back.

"They've bloody started Dave! They're fighting again!"

Dave rushed into the canteen without hesitation, a big carving knife in his hand.

"Right you shower, out of my canteen!" he glared at them. "You want to fight, you do it somewhere else! Now piss off, the lot of you!"

They gave him a few dirty looks before they quickly exited the premises. I was impressed with the chef: he had not blinked. If a big man like Dave had come at me with a carving knife, I too would have quickly got out of his way.

This latest incident instantly made me aware of something in the last few days that had overtaken my thoughts: the idea of getting off this bloody ship as soon as I possibly could. I was truly frightened, and by talking to Jim Roberts, our galley boy, I discovered that he felt the same way. I just wanted to escape this vessel and return to Belfast, but that was pie in the sky: how on earth was I about to achieve that? There was no way that I would walk off a ship again just as I did in France on my last ship. France was comparatively close to home. America certainly was not. I had no aces left up my sleeve.

I decided to make a tentative start by mentioning my intentions to Dave after he had put the knife away. Dave did not bat an eyelid upon hearing of my desire to part company with the ship. He laughed out loud and asked me how I planned to escape. He did not show any surprise at all, which I thought strange: no adverse reaction from him.

"I want to get off this bloody ship, Dave. How do I do it?" I was feeling really brave now.

"You're not sick, Ken," Dave replied, "so your options are very limited." To my surprise once again, Dave did not register any surprise.

"We will talk about this in the morning, Ken, and see what we can do."

I thought that he was joking, but far from it. Dave was deadly serious. That made me wonder, although I quickly put it to the back of my mind. Had Dave been involved in this sort of business before?

As I went to my cabin that night, I had a feeling that the chef would come up with some ideas. I would learn soon enough that Dave knew exactly what to do. The only question was whether I would be willing to go through with it.

Chapter Thirty Four

The Plan

IN THE MORNING David summoned me to his cabin. He had not said a great deal throughout breakfast and appeared quite solemn. This was quite unlike the jovial, carefree, could–not–care–less, could–not–give–a–shit Dave Smith whom I liked and with whom I was familiar.

"Right Ken, what's the story?" he enquired. "You told me right out of the blue that you wanted to part company with this ship." He looked at me sternly. "I intimated that I could possibly help you, and with our heads clear and a cup of tea we will now discuss your options." He paused for a few seconds before continuing. "Are the fighting and all this unrest bothering you?"

"Dead right, Dave - you got it in one," I said. "Nothing will change my mind. I have to go."

Once again, I thought to myself, I have got the homesick blues. I thought I was over that, but this fighting had aggravated the affliction again. The truth was that I would rather be anywhere else than on this ship, a time bomb waiting to go off.

"Right then," Dave said, interrupting my thoughts, "that's plain enough, though I must tell from the start, there is only one option…" We both stared at each other. "I am probably going to shock you. Are you ready for this, Ken?"

"I am Dave," I blurted out quickly, lying. What the hell was he going to say? What if I could not go through with what he had in mind? He came straight to the point:

"You could have an accident where you injure a finger while preparing food." I stared vacantly at him, trying to process what he had told me. "We do cut our fingers when we are cooking from time to time," Dave added.

"That goes with the job, Dave: we put a plaster on the cut and carry on. But that will not get me off the ship."

"What I mean, Ken," said Dave, "and let me be precise: your knife or meat axe will slip and you will cut off a little top joint of one of your fingers…"

"Are you fucking crazy, Dave? I would be in absolute agony!" I was in temporary shock. Dave ignored my outburst.

"While you are thinking about this, let me explain: you will feel very little pain if any at all. I guarantee you this."

"You have done something like this before on another ship, haven't you, Dave?" I asked him nervously. Dave smiled, but before he could answer, I quickly interjected: "Dave, I don't want to know." We sat for a few moments in silence. "I am not sure that I could accurately sever a joint; I would definitely mess it up," I said.

"I will do the deed, Ken," said Dave. "Not you."

"You promise me no pain, Dave?"

"The pain is negligible: this I sincerely promise." This crazy chef has done something like this before, I thought to myself. "Now I must make it clear, Ken: if we go ahead with this then we must stick to the story. Otherwise we will be in trouble."

"You have my word, Dave." It would be sheer stupidity to say anything else. Mind you, I thought to myself, it would be sheer stupidity if I were to go ahead with this farce. "If this comes about Dave, you will be minus a cook."

"I'm not worried about that, Ken," Dave replied. "I will have my own way aboard ship, and anyway they will soon fly out a replacement."

Dave went on to explain that it does not require a large

meat chopper to cut off a joint. I had seen his little personal blade, not much bigger than a knife. He told me that he would get the chippy to sharpen it in order to do the job properly. It was as if he were talking about cutting into a side of beef.

"Now this is how we go about it," Dave went on to say. "You and I will be working in the galley tomorrow evening, preparing a meal for the captain and his guests for the following evening. He will be entertaining the two engineers who have been inspecting the ship's engines."

I remembered the farewell dinner being planned for the two Swedes. They were indeed leaving the ship the following day. The ship's chief engineer and the ship's first officer would also be there. Most of the ship's crew would be ashore. The ship should be bare. Dave was rattling on with details about the plan. He seemed to be really enjoying the logistics of all this.

"Now here is what will happen, Ken. This is the story we will relate." He went on: "While we were preparing a meal for the Captain's dinner, your meat axe slipped off a bone you were using for stock for soup. In a split-second reaction, and acting in self–preservation, your fingers left the chopping board, all except your ring finger and little finger." I listened with perverse fascination. "Your reactions were not quick enough, and in the process the top joint of your ring finger was severed. Your little finger was saved, because of course that was below your ring finger. Simple as that."

"Simple as that for you, Dave," I replied. "What if you miss?"

"I will not miss," Dave stated. "Please be assured of that."

Dave told me to go back to my cabin, have a good sleep and to make my final decision in the morning. He said that if in the end I decided to go ahead with the plan, there was absolutely nothing to worry about. It was alright for him to say there is nothing to worry about: it was not his finger that was coming off, and if it was successful he would be patting himself on the chest. Still, I thought, I should not think like this. I was the one who approached Dave on what I could do to get off this ship and he was willing to put himself out to help me. I would trust his skill with a blade, and he would trust me to stick to the story.

I did not want to think of what the consequences might be and I took to my bed. There would be a long road ahead. The only thing was worrying me at that moment was the loss of my little finger joint. I eventually dropped off to sleep knowing deep down that I would not change my mind.

The next morning I awoke, funnily enough, fully refreshed. I look at my hand and the finger in question. What the hell, it was only a thin little thing.

I was convinced Dave knew what he was doing, and he would assure me once again that a minimum of pain would be experienced. Now I was determined, after this assurance from a man I trusted, to pursue this plan with vigour. Now that the fog was lifting, I could see almost clearly ahead. All the way back home to Belfast. As the famous Beach Boy's song *Sloop John B* goes, let me go home, this is the worst ship I have ever been on.

What Dave told me over lunch removed all doubt. He had just heard that the La Primavera would be staying at sea for at least another year on the Japan to America route, which was expected as it was a tramp steamer, or a ship which could stay at sea for a couple of years if need be and if there was a lucrative market. That was that. Another year on this ship, even if there was no fighting, would not have suited me at all. Now everything was as clear as it could be.

All I could think of was to escape this ship and return to Belfast. In my tunnel vision at that moment, there was only one possible route that would guarantee my immediate exit.

A few drinks, an accident and a trip to hospital…

Chapter Thirty Five

Consequences

THE SHIP IS virtually deserted, Dave observed as we cleared up after dinner. Almost everyone had gone ashore to sample the delights of Portland, whatever they might be. This was it: reality hit me square in the face as Dave started to prepare everything for the so–called accident. The galley workbench was cleared. A very clean, sanitised wooden chopping block was placed on the surface. Dave noticed the sullen grimace on my pallid face.

"Do you realise," Dave asked me with some irony, "that I could be joining them? But I am sacrificing that pleasure to be here with you…"

He made this statement with a huge smile across his face. Fear shot through me at the thought that Dave would rather be here, preparing for my operation like a surgeon; a galley surgeon, to be precise.

"You know what we discussed yesterday, Ken," he reminded me. "You are chopping a bone and the axe slips. Quick reaction saves your fingers with the exception of your ring finger. That is the story."

"I understand perfectly, Dave," I reassured him. "The real story stays with you and me only."

Everything was ready. Dave had a brand new chef's cleaning cloth ready to put around my hand. I had finished my can of beer and was enjoying my first sip of whiskey to give me courage when Dave told me to put my finger on the block. The scary thing was that the chef seemed to be enjoying this.

"Put only your top finger joint on the block," he instructed me.

This was a relief because in my utter naivety I had thought all along that my entire hand would be going on the chopping block. Yes, that made me feel a whole lot better.

"Ken, are you ready?"

"As ready as I will ever be Dave."

The tot of whiskey that I had just finished was definitely helping. I was about to ask for another when Dave spoke.

"Come on Ken. It's only a tiny little piece of finger; you won't notice it gone."

"That is very funny, Dave," I managed to reply in spite of the tremendous trepidation building up inside me before the prospect of bodily mutilation.

Once again Dave asked me if I was ready.

"Yes," was my nervous reply. "Please, do not frigging miss, Dave."

Dave held my hand to make sure it stayed still. The little meat axe which had been honed to the sharpness of a razor blade was raised about six inches only. I closed my eyes and felt a sudden jolt. I opened my eyes. The tip of my finger was nowhere to be seen.

"Where is my bit of finger, Dave?" were my first words after the brief operation.

"Your finger joint landed in the pot of stock, Ken," said Dave. "It jumped in the air on impact and landed safely in the pot. I'm going to let it stay there. It will help give the soup a little extra flavour."

I looked at him and I knew he was not joking. He was deadly serious. I did not go any further down that road and that night I did not touch the soup. I really did not want to know where it stopped on its brief journey. I now had other things on my mind.

It was only a few days later that I realised that perhaps it could have been sewn back on to my finger. Through all this chaos, it suddenly dawned on me that Dave was correct when he had assured me there would hardly be any pain or discomfort. There was only a steady drip of blood.

Dave carefully wrapped my hand in the prepared cloth.

"Right Ken, let's get ready for a trip to hospital," he said. I discovered later that he would not be accompanying me on that journey.

It was round about eight thirty in the evening. We hurried to a couple of officers' cabins but nobody was in. Dave was right: most of the crew were ashore.

"To hell with this!" said Dave. "We will go straight to the captain's quarters."

Dave knocked on the door. The captain was entertaining a couple of guests; he did not seem too happy or compassionate as he stared at my hand covered in a white cloth which was slowly turning red. Dave quickly explained what had happened. The captain immediately got on the ship-to-shore phone.

"An ambulance will arrive in about ten minutes, Mr. Patterson," he told me. "Are you alright?"

"I'm not too bad, sir, not too bad at all."

"From what the chef has told me, if it hadn't been for your quick reactions, the two other fingers would have been severed. Well done!"

Excellent, I thought to myself as I tried to hide a smile: he believes our story. Mission accomplished.

When the ambulance arrived the captain asked Dave to walk me to the vehicle.

"I will see you in a while, Mr. Patterson," said the captain. "Good luck!"

That remark did worry me: did he mean he would see me back on the ship or at the hospital? The hospital, I sincerely hoped.

Dave walked me to the gangplank, where we were met by one of the ambulance men who brought me into the ambulance and had a quick look at my finger.

"That does not look too bad at all," he casually exclaimed. "No need to lie on the bunk, sir. You can sit up."

I was waiting for Dave to get in the ambulance, but he was not going to keep me company. He wished me all the best and that was that. The bloody little shit, I thought, what a pal he was turning out to be; as far as he was concerned his job was done.

Later on I realised that I had been unfair with him. He had given me what I wanted: a way off the ship. It was unfair of me to expect any more.

This ambulance was like a Cadillac. In fact, it was a Cadillac. As we sped off, Dave waved a weak goodbye. The Cadillac did not hang about.

"We are going seven miles, sir, to St. Joseph's Hospital just along the Columbia river."

I did not say anything, but thought it strange that we were not going to a hospital in Portland where the ship was berthed. I was getting fed up with being called "sir" so I told the man my name. From that moment on he did not stop talking until we reached the hospital.

Saint Joseph's Hospital, Vancouver, Washington State

"Where are you from, Ken?"

"I'm from Ireland."

"Oh my", he shouted to his mate, the driver. "This young man is from the Emerald Isle, where my wife's folks come from!"

141

And that is all he talked about, from when we started our journey to when we arrived at the hospital. Never once did he mention my finger again.

We arrived at about nine thirty, and another phase in my latest escape from a ship was about to begin.

Chapter Thirty Six

Needlework

ONE OF THE ambulance men led me to reception at St. Joseph's Hospital, where they took my name. We were met by a nurse who escorted me to what looked like a small operating theatre designed for minor treatments. There I was met by a sister who brought me to a chair and told me to sit down. Nobody had bothered to ask me about my bloody finger.

After about five minutes an old chap dressed in a suit comes in and draws up a chair opposite me.

"Good evening, young man! What is your name?"

"Kenneth Patterson, Doctor."

"Well, Kenneth Patterson, I am Dr. Robinson and I will be attending to your finger."

They already knew about my injury courtesy of radio ambulance to hospital.

"Shall I take the young man's clothes off, Doctor?" asked the nurse.

"No, Sister; there is no need for that," he replied.

"Have you ever watched your mother sewing?"

"Yes, I have," I said.

"Well then you can watch me sew because that is what I am about to do. And do not worry; you will not feel a thing."

I was not reassured by that remark, although I was not too sure that I would enjoy the experience to come.

Dr. Robinson injected the base of my finger at the front and then again at the rear base of my finger. I did not feel any pain, but then he had not started sewing yet.

"We will wait a couple of minutes for the injections to work, and then we will start sewing."

Not once did he mention the word stitch. His manner of speaking was so nonchalant that you would think he was about to sew a button on a shirt, but then he must have carried out this procedure dozens of times. I hoped so anyway. It was not a life threatening operation, but his informality did not set me entirely at ease.

After about five minutes, he asked me if I was ready but did not wait for my reply. The bedside manner did not apply to this old geezer. He prodded my finger with a needle.

"Can you feel that?"

"Feel what?" I courageously replied.

"Here we go."

I watched as he put a needle right through my finger and expertly began to close the gap with a few stitches. I thought I was in a dream because I felt no pain, just a little discomfort. This guy, for all his flamboyance, was pretty darn good at a spot of darning.

"Put a tight sling on, Sister, take him to his bed, and then you can help to take his clothes off." Then he looked at me. "Before you go, young man, I will see you in a couple of days to check your finger. If it looks alright, if the stitches have taken, I will be back again in a few days to remove them."

Was I hearing things? He more or less said I would be in hospital for at least a week. The ship would sail at the latest in two days. The captain was not going to delay the departure because of little old me. I went to sleep eventually that night, in a crisp, clean alluring bed, feeling at least cautiously optimistic.

I awakened the next morning and realised that I was laid on a bed on land and not on a ship. After a breakfast of waffles and syrup, I looked around me and to my surprise saw that I was in a very small ward which seemed more like a large living room. But then this was not a NHS hospital: this was America and as I was to learn later this was a private hospital. This doctor was going to make a few dollars out of my incarceration. To my delight I concluded that he would keep me in here as long as he could.

There were three patients in my little ward and that included me. I was reading a morning paper when I encountered a shadow standing over me. It was one of the inmates.

"Excuse me, please," he said. "Sorry to interrupt. I would like to introduce myself and welcome you to our ward." He spoke as if it were a hotel rather than a hospital. "My name is Jason Smith. Are you well?"

"My name is Ken Patterson, and I am well, Mr. Smith."

"Well, Ken, I am in here with a broken arm as you can see."

I looked up and indeed his arm was in a sling; he was wearing silk pyjamas with an expensive looking silk dressing gown.

"I cut a bit of my finger off, Jason," I explained. "I was a cook on a ship anchored in Portland."

"Oh dear, that's unfortunate. They will sail without you. I detect an Irish accent, sir; how lovely to meet someone from Ireland!"

"You detected right, Jason."

I tried to get off this Irish thing by changing the subject straightaway and asking him where he came from.

"I hail from Portland, Ken," Jason explained. "I own a chicken farm on the outskirts of the city."

Lunch was about to be served and so ended our conversation. I spent the rest of the day reading local newspapers and sleeping.

I awakened the next morning on day two, and after breakfast, Jason and I were conversing again. He asked me if was I enjoying the food, and whether I liked the nurses.

That was strange. I had only seen a nurse on one occasion. Then Jason Smith said something which took me aback: he asked me if I would I like to work on his farm.

This made me slightly uneasy; he was virtually a complete stranger and I knew absolutely nothing about him. How was I going to get out of this one?

"I don't think so, Jason," was my reply. "For a start the authorities would not wear that at all: an alien seaman working and putting down roots in your country without any papers."

Hopefully that would have put him off. But he was a determined American.

Late that afternoon, Jason sauntered over to my bed again.

"I'm sorry, Ken."

"What are you sorry for, Jason?"

"Well, I am sorry to tell you that I have been in touch with American Immigration and they have informed me that under no circumstances would you be allowed to stay and work in America."

Jason might have been sorry, but I certainly was not. I thanked him ever so much for trying, but could not believe that this comparative stranger had actually been in touch with his country's immigration authorities concerning the possibility of my working in America. I thought this man was joking from the very start when he first mentioned the prospect of working on his chicken farm.

I tried to avoid Mr. Smith from that moment on by going for a dander around the hospital, coming back and pretending to be asleep. I had other things on my mind.

I had been going over the fighting on the ship, my thinking of ways to get off it, and the caper of the chef's amputating part of my finger. I had not been thinking of the future at all; I was existing day by day. Luckily everything seemed to be working out so far, and I could at long last gather my thoughts and start thinking about the future for a change.

I went to bed that night and once thought more of Jason Smith's attempts to allow me the opportunity to work in America. Was this man a pervert or just a generous soul? What were his motives? And I had foolishly given him my address in Belfast. What was I thinking of?

What I did not know at the time, and was to discover a few months later, much to my shame, was that Jason Smith was being considerably kind and thoughtful to a stranger in his country. This man, for the next three years, was to send me a single dollar bill as a gesture of friendship to my address in Belfast on my birthday.

Sadly in the world as it was then and has become, the kindness of strangers is mistaken for some ulterior motive, when in fact it is just what it is: the kindness of strangers.

Chapter Thirty Seven

Escape

O N THE MORNING of my third day in hospital, Dr. Robinson paid me a visit. He placed two chairs in the middle of the ward, like he did when he was sewing my finger.

"Let's have a look at that finger, young man." The sister took off the dressing. "Sure looks good to me, Mr. Patterson," he added. "The stitches have taken well. We should have them out in two or three days' time."

He told the sister to put a clean dressing on and off he went as quickly as he came; busy man, money to be made.

After Dr. Robinson's visit, I laid back on my bed reading a newspaper. I looked up and there was the captain of the La Primavera, looking at me.

"Good morning, sir," I managed to choke out.

"Good morning to you, Mr. Patterson," he replied. "I have come to say goodbye. We are slightly behind our schedule, but I thought I would come and see you before we sail. To tell you the truth, I was hoping you would be well enough to join the ship, but that is not to be. I spoke to your doctor and he informed me that under no circumstances would you be leaving hospital in the next few days."

I inwardly breathed a sigh of relief.

"By the way," the captain went on to say, "you are not the only casualty staying behind: Mr. Roberts, your colleague, the galley boy, is in hospital in Portland."

This did take me by surprise. Jim Roberts was the 'peggy', the galley boy, the young lad who washed the pots and pans and was a general dogsbody on call for whatever menial jobs needed to be done at the behest of the chef. He was a gaunt wee fellow who I did not think would last long in the Merchant Navy, in all my wisdom. He was a quiet, forlorn character of few words, normally.

"What's wrong with him?" I managed to utter.

"Well, he had severe pains in his stomach a couple of days ago and was rushed to hospital with suspected appendicitis. Tests were carried out and they suspected a grumbling appendix. As it is, he will be under observation for another two to three days, and if things are well, it looks like he will be joining you when you leave hospital. I have already paid a visit to Mr. Roberts."

"I will visit him as soon as I can, sir," I said.

"Well, I must go. Good luck! You will be home before long."

Off he went. That was the last I saw of the captain of La Primavera. The way he had said "you will be home before long" made me wonder if he suspected anything, but I thought that this was probably my imagination.

I could not believe the way that this had turned out and actually let out a shout of joy. Bloody brilliant! No doubts anymore: that ship was definitely sailing without me. Not only that, but I would also have some company in the form of Jim Roberts. According to the captain, the shipping company's shipping agent would collect us from outside the hospital and deliver us to our hotel when we were discharged.

After three days, I felt that Dr. Robinson was really stringing this out. Once again he put me on a chair, looked at my finger now completely closed and healed. The stitches had taken well; his mother would be proud of her son's sewing. He proceeded to take them out and that was the only time I felt a little pain during the saga of my missing digit.

"Well, young man, you are free to go," said the doctor. "Sister, will you please put a sling on his arm. There is a chap waiting in reception who is going to take you to your hotel in Portland."

"Thank you, Doctor, for your trouble."

"No trouble at all, son," he replied. I bet it was not, I thought to myself. The shipping company would have a hefty bill, but that was not my concern.

I gathered my few belongings, met the agent in reception, stepped into his car and we were on our way to Portland. Ten minutes later we were in the hotel, where I would stay until passage home.

Booked in at reception there was a beaming Jim Roberts waiting for me. We shook hands, had a quick hug and you could not stop us talking. The agent managed to interrupt us with a few dollars in his hand.

"You boys will get a breakfast and a meal at dinner time in the hotel. I have been authorised to give you each a dollar a day to get a burger or whatever at lunchtime. The receptionist will give you the money every day."

That was enough in the days ahead to buy a hamburger and a coffee, although we did discover a preference for the doughnut shops whose fare was delicious.

The agent bade us goodbye, said he would drop by in a couple of days to see if we were settling in alright, and after that would come when he had news of departure from America. That suited us fine. We knew we would be going home soon and in the meantime we would relax and laze about in the Pacific Northwest of the United States of America.

Jim would tell me nearly every day of the joy he felt, the relief of getting off that bloody ship. He told me that it was worth the pain and the agony to be back on dry land and away from those troublemakers. All in all we had both came out of it well. I too was relieved to be off that ship; as far as I was concerned I had been in a tough spot. What would have happened had I not had my 'accident'? I do not know, but I do know what I did out of desperation and how, apart from my loss, it had turned out well. I was glad to be off a ship where there could be, and I do not exaggerate, civil unrest, Catholics and Protestants fighting, and a chef who was losing his faculties and slowly going mad. His personality had changed greatly, from carefree when we set sail to depressive on the open sea. We agreed that another one or two years aboard that ship would have finished us off. We wanted home: we did not mention it to each other but part of our trouble was homesickness.

When we least expect it, light will always pierce the darkness. Life is a bitter sweet web of emotions: sadness, joy, elation, happiness and, last but not least, hope.

Hope is crucial. In the last few weeks I had experienced all of these feelings in a way that I was sure would never have been possible if I had stayed in Belfast. But Belfast was pulling me back, all the same...

Chapter Thirty Eight

Jim and the Cowboy

I WILL LOOK after you two English boys," said the cook in our hotel. He was a young ex–marine and obviously did not recognise our Northern Irish accents, which was a relief: unlike the case with the two ambulance men and Jason Smith from the hospital, this time we did not have to answer dozens of questions. He was not going to mention Galway bay, the Ring of Kerry and the mountains of Mourne sweeping down to the sea. Fair enough though, that young man did feed us well: pancakes with maple syrup, crispy bacon and as he put it, eggs over easy.

Most days, Jim and I would sit in the hotel foyer which was occupied by old people, and every day they were completely obsessed with detective films on the hotel television. This establishment was really a glorified B&B. It was certainly not The Ritz; a bit scruffy and rough around the edges. Well, I am ungrateful; let us say that it was well worn, like a welcoming abode. At the same time, it felt like a nursing home, although there were no zombies running around. I believe if one of the guests were taken sick, they would be dispatched to a hospital. The ones who remained would spend the rest of their days in the hotel.

Jim and I sometimes felt a little uneasy because we were the only two young people in the hotel. This did seem a bit strange, but this feeling did not last long simply because these elderly people went out of their way to be welcoming and friendly to the two young strangers who had invaded their hotel. These kindly people always seemed to me to be in a state of utopia, and I suppose that that is a fine state to be in.

One evening, on impulse and out of boredom, Jim and I ventured into a tavern which was conveniently situated about ten yards from our hotel. It was a typical American establishment, the same as you would see in an American film: a long sweeping bar with the obligatory and numerous bar stools.

Jim Roberts and I were not of the legal age to consume alcohol in America, but we decided to try our luck anyway. All the barman could do was to refuse our custom, but he did not, so we ordered two beers. This was big time for us two scruffs in an American pub, drinking with the big boys. We sat there like we owned the place, becoming really confident.

We heard the door squeak. It swings open, Jim and I look round, and in danders this giant of a man, plonks himself on a stool beside Jim and orders a beer. This guy really looked like a cowboy. We had seen cowboys in the films that we watched back home, but had never seen one in the flesh.

Of course, he was not a cowboy, but my imagination really did run riot for a few moments. I looked at Jim and noticed that the colour had left his face for a few seconds; he was twitching, probably wishing that this big man had jumped on a stool next to me.

"Howdy folks!" shouts the cowboy and orders his second beer. This giant had a Stetson on his head, a waistcoat, and a gun tucked into a holster round his waist.

"Excuse me, sir," Jim piped up, "but are you a cowboy?"

Jim's inquisitiveness made me very nervous and I was getting ready to run.

"Hell no, boy," replied the man. "I'm just an ordinary all-night truck driver."

With his next question, Jim really made me twitch.

"If you are not a cowboy, mister, could I ask you why you are carrying a gun?"

"Well, I will tell you why, boy: I wear it for protection. Now and again one of our trucks gets held up, and most of the time the guys that do this are mean, and think nothing of shooting a driver to get the contents of the truck. A lot of the time these bandits know exactly what we are transporting."

This seemed to satisfy my friend's curiosity, and he thanked the trucker. I nudged Jim and told him it was time to go. He took the hint. We said our goodbyes and vacated the premises as quickly as we could. I decided that that would be the last time I would buy Jim a beer, and we went back to our cosy little life in the hotel.

The next morning at breakfast we had our waffles and honey washed down with a couple of cups of coffee. We were getting used to this American food. That afternoon we went to a cinema to watch the beautiful Elizabeth Taylor in a film called Butterfield 8.

The cinema was clean, comfortable and modern with fast food in abundance. My thoughts took me back to my childhood visits to the Lyceum Cinema where only ice cream was on offer. As much as we were enjoying our easy, laid back life in Portland, I for one was more than ever dreaming of home. I was, of course, homesick and longing to see old Belfast again, the city from which I had yearned to escape.

Little did I know it, but that dream was about to come true in the next couple of days.

Chapter Thirty Nine

Mister Sims and Ms. Jane Russell

MONDAY MORNING; THE tenth day of our stay in this hotel. Jim and I were becoming weary and bored. A departure would be most welcome. I have always referred to the hotel as this hotel or that hotel; I never did see a name.

Perhaps it was a nursing home; after all, it was occupied by old people who just watched television day and night and in between mealtimes.

Jim and I had just finished our breakfast. A meal of fresh bacon and eggs: a welcome change from bloody waffles. We brought our third cup of coffee into the foyer. I don't think the beverage tea had reached America yet, at least not on a large, popular scale.

"Good morning, chaps," was the greeting which reached our ears as we went to sit down.

Before we could utter a good morning in return, Mr. Sims, the shipping agent, looked at me and blurted out, "I'm about to make your day, Mr. Patterson."

"What about making my day?" Jim retorted.

Mr. Sims ignored this outburst from Jim, and continued with a big grin on his face:

"You will be on your way home starting on Wednesday. You will be joining the ship Colorado Star of the Blue Star line."

"Whoa, whoa, whoa!" Jim shouts out, "I have not heard my name mentioned here – have I missed out on something?"

"Mr. Roberts, let me explain," Sims told a scowling Jim. "There is only one spare cabin on the Colorado Star, and a very small one at that, so only one of you can make this trip…"

"Why can't I go, then?" asked Jim. "I'm younger than Ken and…"

Sims interrupted him, saying, "Well now, that's the whole point: you have just put your finger on it. Our policy is seniority. Let me explain. Mr. Patterson is senior to you in rank and length of service. He is a second cook and baker; you are a galley boy. You have just joined the Merchant Navy. Mr. Patterson, on the other hand, has been in a lot longer."

This perfectly worded explanation did not appease Jim at all and he was to sulk for the rest of the day. He did pick up though when the agent told him he would be joining a ship heading home on Saturday.

I knew what was annoying Jim: he did not want to be on his own for the next two or three days. I told him to read a book, watch the television and Saturday will arrive before you realise it. He seemed to calm down then.

I could understand the way he was feeling; I would not fancy being on my own in this hotel without a name, even if it were only for a brief period.

The day before, after finishing my breakfast, I took a newspaper from the hotel's reception and read the disturbing news that a fourteen-year old boy had attempted to decapitate his mother and father as they slept in their bed. They were rushed to hospital at death's door. After finishing reading such grisly headlines, I was even more relieved and grateful at the prospect of shipping out on Wednesday morning and beginning the voyage home.

However, after reading about the horrors that could take place in this vast, colourful country, where truckers dressed as cowboys and wearing huge Stetsons carried guns and complete strangers offered you employment, I glanced out of the window of my hotel room and captured the sight of the beautiful actress Jane Russell. She was hurrying, fleetingly, from her nearby hotel, along the sidewalk to an awaiting car.

Did I really see that curvaceous, buxom and glamourous figure from American cinema? Yes, I did.

Actress Jane Russell

We know instinctively when we have set eyes on someone who is well known, in the public eye or famous. I knew it was her then, and I remain convinced today that it was the much-publicised screen siren.

I had no idea at the time what she was doing in Portland, Oregon, and today am none the wiser. Her film career at that time was in the middle of a seven year hiatus, and she would not star in another production until 1964. During this period she worked the nightclub circuit with a solo act and performed in the theatre with roles in drama and musicals.

Who knows what brought an instantly-recognisable figure from Hollywood to that city in the Pacific Northwest, and what were the chances that during those few seconds an unknown, fresh-faced wanderer such as myself would look out of his window and see something that lit up his day and that he would never forget?

In but a few seconds my mind had hurtled from horror to beauty. A distraction, a delay or some other misplacement of time and that memory would never have come into existence.

"I'll pick you up at nine o' clock on Wednesday morning, Mr. Patterson," said Sims. "The ship sails round about noon, giving you plenty of time to settle in." He looked at Jim. "I'll sort you out later, Mr. Roberts. Goodbye until Wednesday!"

From the time he met us to the time that I left, Jim had been miserable most of the time. I had a feeling Mr. Sims would be glad to see the back of us.

Wednesday came like a shot. Sims picked me up spot on at nine o'clock. I said my goodbyes to a sad looking Jim and waved to a couple of the hotel prisoners. We drove through Portland as quickly as was legally allowed and arrived at the ship in ten minutes. We walked up the gangplank. Sims introduced me to a couple of crew members, wished me a good trip and said goodbye. I was shown to my cabin by a crew member about a couple of years older than me. He was a very friendly and welcoming fellow. The shipping agent was not wrong when he had explained to an irritable Jim that the cabin was extremely small: there was just about enough room to swing the proverbial cat in it.

In the next few days I was to find these crew members very friendly; they made me feel welcome and treated me like a passenger, which is what I essentially was on that voyage. They very different to a few of the crew I had left on the La Primavera. What a relief!

Two or three of the crew were of my age, two were deck and one was catering. These three lads and I became good friends in the days to follow. All they wanted to know was what had happened to my finger and what it was like on my last ship.

This ship would be making a stop at Stockton for a couple of hours to pick up a few food supplies, and then on to Long Beach to take on cargo, and then home. I would be visiting California again.

We sailed at noon under a glorious blue cloudless sky. I had lunch, retired to my cabin, sorted out my few belongings and retired for the night.

I was not proud of myself for the injury that had been done to my finger, but I was determined not to dwell on it for too long. It was a means to an end and borne of desperation and fear. I was learning how easy it always is to recognise mistakes on hindsight. I had done something foolish out of panic, and had learned the valuable lesson never to do that again.

These and a thousand other thoughts swirled and ebbed around in my mind as the familiar, comforting sounds of a ship on the ocean at night ushered me towards the bliss of sleep.

Chapter Forty

Homeward

A COUPLE OF days and over five hundred miles later, we arrived in Stockton. The weather was good, the journey was uneventful.

Stockton is in San Joaquin County and has the largest inland seaport on the West Coast. The schedule was to be a couple of hours in port, but due to other circumstances we were told that the ship would be lying overnight. This suited us fine, and my new found friends and I decided to take advantage of the situation with an evening trip into town after dinner. We came upon a cinema, which was incidentally the smallest cinema that I have ever seen, and decided to go in to see a film that had not long been released: The Alamo starring John Wayne and Richard Widmark.

Historical accuracy did not get much of a look in with this epic Hollywood version of the famous and heroic defence in Texas. John Wayne as Davy Crockett kills single–handedly dozens of Mexican troops as his small band of patriots holds out against a vastly superior army. Unfortunately, there was much tedious horseplay and moralising to endure at the beginning, but the film really took off once the shooting started.

We enjoyed the film and were with Davy Crockett all the way, as was the audience of yanks surrounding us. We got excited quietly, but the yanks let rip and started being very vocal once Davy started shooting.

Early next morning we headed for Long Beach and arrived a couple of days later.

Long Beach, a city in Los Angeles County, has one of the biggest shipping ports in America if not the world, and that was where we were berthed. The ship was there to pick up cargo, and depart in a few days, but once again we overstayed. We ended up being there for three days.

My mates told me that they had made the trip to Long Beach before and had enjoyed their stay. They went on to tell me that they had taken a trip on the largest big dipper in the world. I could sense where this was leading and after lunch my mates invited me to join them on an excursion into town.

As soon as we entered town, they asked me to join them for a trip on the big dipper. I knew I should have stayed on the ship, but I could not get out of this one. I reluctantly agreed.

We paid our money and took our seats on the roller coaster. Before we took off, I glanced up and the top of the roller coaster looked extremely high, and I mean extremely high. I was cursing myself for agreeing to this.

Paddy and Sean were sat in front of me; I was on my bloody own sat behind them. The bastards had planned this all along.

Off we went, picked up speed, up into the sky, then down. These two in front of me from the start did not hold the bar: they had their hands up all through the ride.

I, on the other hand, was holding on and gripping the safety bar for dear life.

These so–called mates looked over their shoulders at me several times, laughing their heads off at my distress. I was so relieved when that journey was over.

It had been a very scary experience and I resolved never to ride on a big dipper ever again, a resolution I never managed to uphold.

On the third morning of our Stockton berth we set sail for Ireland by means of the Panama Canal once again. We slipped out of port and were on our way. I would help out unofficially in the galley with a spot of cooking sometimes to break the monotony.

The Panama Canal would be in sight in four or five days. It would take several hours to go through the canal and then on to the Atlantic.

We made it to the Panama Canal without a skirmish. The heat that we endured whilst going through the canal was stifling, and working in the galley did not help.

The Panama Canal is a great American feat of engineering in the twentieth century, and moves ships over a continental divide that separates two oceans. Every inch of the fifty-mile long, man-made channel is surrounded by breath-taking natural beauty and I went on deck to marvel at this whenever I could, gasping for air in the heat.

It took us about nine hours to transit the canal, and by nightfall we were cruising upon the Atlantic.

After lunch I would walk up to the poop deck, strip to my trunks and enjoy the sun every day for the twenty or so days back to Belfast. As far as I was concerned, I was treated as a guest. I was enjoying myself, would never see the La Primavera again and was content.

As I felt the sun's rays on me, I had nothing to see but the future. The journey back to Britain was uneventful; no rough seas and a bright blue sky all the way.

Early in the afternoon on a rainy September day the Colorado Star docked in Belfast. What a wonderful feeling: back in old Belfast after being away for such a long time. The familiar sight of the giant cranes of Harland and Wolff were there to welcome me again, and in the distance the Cavehill and Napoleon's Nose rising above the city.

I gathered my few belongings, said goodbye to a few mates, and with a spring in my step started the walk to my house, feeling like a returning hero. I took my old familiar route, leaving the docks, crossing over York Street and over North Queen Street, a quarter mile on and on to the New Lodge Road. Nothing had changed: it was as if I had never been away.

Half an hour later I knocked on the door of my home in Singleton Street. I had been away for ten months, had travelled thousands of miles and seen quite a lot of the world. The prodigal son had returned.

My father answered the door and stared at me incredulously for about five seconds.

"Is it yourself, Ken?"

"Indeed it is, Da."

I could understand why my father was initially confused: I had left home with a pale complexion and hair in a short crew cut style, and now this stranger was stood at the door with a deep brown complexion and hair down to his shoulders.

I waited that afternoon until everyone was home and then proceeded to tell them of my time at sea. I also mentioned my finger and the missing joint. I told them a white lie of how it had been an accident. My family accepted this and never questioned it.

After everyone had gone to bed my mother and I drank cups of tea until the early hours of the morning as we had often done before. She told me a couple of lads had joined the army, a couple of others had found work in England and my cousin Beatrice had immigrated to Canada.

Apart from that, she said nothing had changed; everything had stayed the same.

Little did I know it then, but things were going to change and would never be the same again. In a few short months I would be joining the R.A.F. for a five year engagement. This would lead to further escapades abroad.

I would be able to revive my love of boxing.

I would forge new friendships and find new comrades.

Sometimes I would barely escape with my life.

I am retired now as I finish writing about this part of my life. But I am not the age I am. I can still do what I want to do regardless of what the numbers tell me.

Growing old is not a disease; it is a part of life. So I almost always act young, think young, and find that this approach certainly works.

In my youth I made mistakes and did some stupid, irresponsible things. But I was single and responsible only to myself. I never did hurt or harm anyone else, which make the memories of such mistakes not entirely bad and even the source of laughter now.

I have a simple philosophy in life: to be old and wise, you must first be young and foolish.

After a few weeks back in Belfast, the young and foolish I began to feel a familiar twitch, a niggling, a restlessness. Yes, by now I knew that feeling as well as I knew its polar opposite, homesickness.

It was time to wander again...

And this is where Ken's story began…

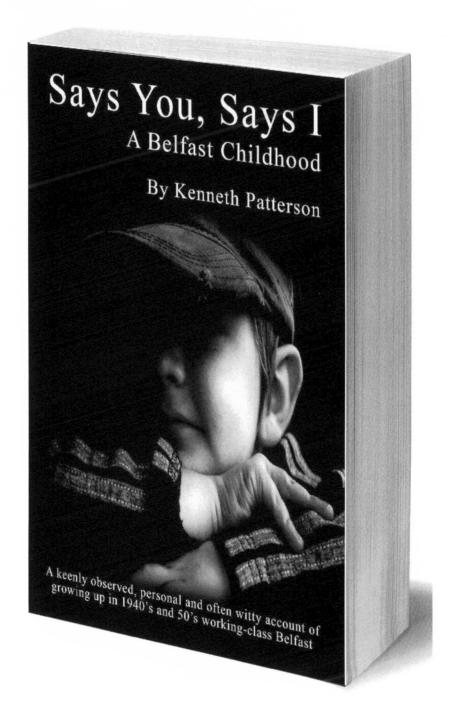

ONE

Starting off

I entered this world approximately two minutes after midnight on March 18th 1942, weighing in at a princely eight pounds. Had I been born on the other side of midnight, my Mother told me that she would have named me Patrick. Over the years I have been truly grateful that she christened me Ken: being called Paddy would not have suited me at all.

Unlike a couple of my siblings, my birth was straightforward. Throughout my life, from a young boy to the day my Mother died, I never gave her cause for concern. I adored and loved her unconditionally, and believe that I was her favourite as she was mine. I was the fourth of five children: three boys, two girls. My Father was in the Air Force at this time, and stationed at Aldergrove in Northern Ireland. I was born in Crumlin, a little village in County Antrim.

We moved to Belfast at the end of the war, into a little two–up two–down terraced house. Seven of us in our family, five children and Ma and Da, and crammed into this little dolls house, made life very uncomfortable at times. We had a very tiny outside toilet in a very tiny back yard with whitewashed walls. I remember when I was older, on a summer's day, helping my Da to paint those walls.

Funnily enough, I enjoyed that. Our toilet paper was the News of the World and the Sunday People newspapers, cut into neat squares and hung on a piece of string attached to a big rusty nail on the brick toilet wall. Although we could not afford proper toilet paper, I could sit on my toilet seat, read the newspaper and then wipe my arse with it.

Instead of having to bring the paper back in to the house with me, it was flushed down the toilet, and the headlines or the sports page or a saucy story were imprinted on my backside. Not many people nowadays can perform that trick.

In the summer it was a pleasant experience, enjoyable even, being sat on the outside toilet. Apart from the odd fly tickling your arse and a wasp going in for the attack, it was bearable enough. Yet with the onset of winter and the dark cold nights, it was hell sometimes, especially when the snow was lying on the ground.

I slipped a few times in the snow, going that short distance to the toilet. If you didn't break your neck, you could freeze to death: it all depended how long you were on the toilet seat. If it was a short session you were alright. If it was diarrhoea, then you were literally in the shits. You would be on the seat for such a long time that paralysis would set in.

The most important thing to remember in the winter was to keep your hands warm, otherwise you would not have the strength to give your arse a good wipe. What's more, you did not have the luxury of a shower or a bath after this horrendous experience.

Until your tin bath came up once a week, you were stuck with the newspaper headlines all over your backside. Proper toilet paper was an expensive and rare commodity when I was a boy. You can imagine what a trip to the toilet was like in the winter, especially a Belfast winter: extremely cold and uncomfortable, not to mention the newspaper which the skin rejected most of the time.

Our kitchen consisted of a gas cooker (second hand), a kitchen cabinet, in which all our food, butter, milk, potatoes etc. were kept. The other item was a large square sink. That sink was used for washing dishes, washing clothes (underpants included) and washing all us kids. There was no running hot water; occasionally a kettle was put on the stove for us kids to have a wash in the kitchen sink. Everything and everybody was washed in that old sink. I well remember on a Monday, when my Mother would always do the washing, helping her to rinse and wring the clothes under the ice cold water running from the water tap in the sink. The pain in your hands from the running cold water was almost unbearable; in the summer it was not too bad, but in the winter it was child cruelty. Of course, after the water was wrung from the clothes in the kitchen, I would then follow my Ma into the little wintry backyard and proceed to turn the handle of the clothes mangle while she pushed the clothes through the rollers. I had the toughest job turning that bloody handle, but I insisted on the toughest job, as I was too much of a gentleman to let my mother do it.

Saturday night was the night of the week when we luxuriated in lovely hot water, although when it came to my turn it was bloody freezing. Of course I am talking about the ritual of the Saturday night bath. The tin tub was carried from the backyard through to the little lounge, water was warmed on the gas cooker and everyone took turns to have a weekly scrub. Needless to say when my turn came around, the water was black, cold and stinking.

The kitchen floor was covered in lino, but you could feel the coldness of the concrete underneath. As a boy I remember being on my hands and knees helping my mother to scrub it every day. Our little lounge was more comfortable, and again there was lino on the floor. There was a sofa, a sofa chair, four hard chairs and a table. No radio, no television: it would be years before these luxuries invaded our lives. The best part of our little lounge was the coal fire: we would all huddle round that fire in the cold winter nights. Apart from helping my Ma scrub the kitchen floor and turn the mangle handle, I always seemed to have the honour of cleaning and lighting that bloody dirty fire. I often now wonder if I really was the favourite... We had a separate parlour next to the living room with a little coal fire. The fire was rarely lit, and the room was only used on special occasions, for the occasional birthday party or for my older sister to entertain the odd boyfriend, away from young prying eyes: it was an unwritten rule in our house that a knock on the parlour door was required before gaining entry. At least in this little house one room guaranteed privacy.

Imagine this: two bedrooms upstairs for seven people. Ma and Da in the back room and the five of us roughing it in the front room which had two beds, and we are not talking big double beds either: one was a big single and the other a small double. We used to change sleeping arrangements regularly: one would sleep on the sofa downstairs, upstairs two girls in one bed, and there would be two boys in one bed. Looking back over the years, I realised how impoverished we were, how little we had, living from day to day, mouth to mouth; but we were born into this life style and as far as we were concerned everyone lived like this.

Work was scarce and a lot of men were on the dole. I remember my Mother telling me, while my Father was signing on (with a family of five to feed and clothe), that if there were any benefits from the dole, they would not have sustained us for long). So my Da would borrow a ladder and chamois and go round cleaning windows. He was frequently chased by officials from street to street, trying to catch him working while he was drawing dole. They never did catch him: the neighbours would watch out for the officials and tip off the old man. One neighbour would grab the ladders, enabling my Da to dash to the house and have a cup of tea in his hand when the officials came to call. But life was harsh for my Mother. Although there were quite a few families worse off than us, I cannot begin to imagine how soul destroying it must have been to raise five children in abject poverty. The amazing thing is my Mother achieved this with dignity and I cannot ever remember having an empty belly. My Mother told me her hair was completely grey by the time that she was about twenty five. I don't know if this was hereditary or through worry: the latter would be my guess.

I know that my mother, like most mothers, was always in debt trying to clothe and feed us. But my Mother made sure, and it was her top priority, that her children were fed on as regular a basis as was possible. We had free school dinners and this did help, but I remember my Mother always baking. My Mother was a good baker, and after our bath on a Saturday night, we would all tuck into her beef pies. Sometimes this would be followed by her famous apple pie and custard: little pleased the innocent in those days.

Just after my fourth birthday my Mother delivered me to school. What was going on here? I didn't ask her to take me to school: I was enjoying myself at home. My baby sister and I were getting all of my Ma's attention all day every day, at least until the others came home from school. Now I was about to be separated from my Mother and put into an alien world with a lot of strange children. I knew immediately that this was not for me, and from that moment on, I had a love–hate relationship with school. That is, I loved to hate it.

Meeting Ms. McLean the Headmistress for the first time confirmed this. This wasn't a sweet old lady who was going to make me feel good about being separated from my Ma for the first time in my short life. On the contrary, the exact opposite: the headmistress was an awesome sight to this small child. She looked like a giant, with muscles bulging everywhere, and armed with a massive wooden pointed cane which she held in a tightly clenched, heavily–veined fist. Ms McLean, without further ceremony, deposited me on a seat quite close to the side entrance in Shandon Street, the street next to mine: Singleton Street. About five minutes after my Mother left me, I decided to make a break for freedom when the giant was at the blackboard and her back was toward me. I leapt out of the door into Shandon Street like a bat out of hell and headed for my house which was about a hundred yards from the school.

I was just about to bolt into our street when I was slung into the air and over the shoulder of one of our local dustbin men. Anyway, the bin man gave me to Ma who thanked him and promptly delivered me back to the jailer.

After that episode I remember at least five other aborted attempts at escape, and despite my tearful pleas to Ma, she always quickly brought me back to school and a waiting headmistress quickly running out of patience. Because of this, and the fact that the head warden was about to start using her cane, I decided to knuckle down and be a good boy. That, after all, was what everyone wanted. ˙

From the first day I started school to the day I left, my main priority was to get out of the school gates as soon as lessons ended. Go home, get my banana, sugar or treacle sandwich, glass of milk or buttermilk, or cup of tea, and sail through my homework as quickly as possible without bodging it, because my Ma always checked it: this was the one condition that she imposed upon me before I was allowed to go out and play with my friends.

Once I was out, my Ma would never see me until it was time to come home for tea, and then after tea I was out again until bedtime. We didn't have television in those days, and if your family was poor a radio was never heard of either: hence the reason why we were always out playing; but my parents knew where we were, and they knew that we were safe.

I lived in a street which was one of about ten streets which all led on to the New Lodge Road. Everyone knew everyone in those days and a neighbour would have reported to my Mother had we been seen wandering too far from our neighbourhood. Nowadays, children watch television and mope around the house when they come home from school; they never seem to play outdoors as much as we children did, but then again we didn't have television or even a radio when we were young. What you didn't have, you didn't miss.

As people of my generation will tell you, paedophiles, child abusers, rapists and muggers, were terms that weren't familiar to us and I expect that is why we had so much freedom. School was a place one had to attend: that was the law, but most of the time I never really enjoyed my schooldays. Part of the reason for this was because most of us kids back then were not encouraged by the teachers to achieve academically at school. Despite this drawback, I did get up early one morning, had a rare bacon and egg sandwich and a mug of hot tea to prepare me for the forthcoming exams that I was about to sit that day for an entrance into grammar school, which I knew that I could have passed had I applied myself. Instead I took the easy option, didn't go, met up with a friend, spent my dinner money on sweets and that was that: no commitment, no ambition.

Then again, had I have taken the exam, been successful and offered a place at grammar school, my parents wouldn't have been able to afford it. The reason for this is because when you came from a large family, a starkly poor family, with your parents struggling to clothe you and put food on the table, grammar school and further education was never a topic of conversation: not even a remote option. What was important to parents of impoverished families was for each child at home to leave school at the permitted age and become a bread winner as quickly as possible. I have often regretted leaving school. I have often regretted hating school and often wished that I had gone to grammar school, but this wasn't an option and wouldn't have worked out to everyone's satisfaction.

Truancy was virtually unheard of throughout my schooldays, and it wasn't tolerated by most parents and the Authorities. There seemed to be school inspectors everywhere, and time off school for whatever reason would guarantee a house call by one of them. Bullying was not tolerated either: it wasn't prevalent and wasn't accepted by parents or by teachers. My Mother, any mother, would be on the doorstep of any persistent bully. My way of dealing with them was to get to know one of the so–called hard men of the school, and with a little subservience and a few sweets, your new mate would make sure bullies never bothered you again. Of course, any bullying or fighting would only occur at the secondary schools.

I managed to get through infant school without mishap and then went on to Hillman Elementary School. This was the in–between school, the school between infants and secondary school: the leaving school. Nothing major happened there, except that I noticed girls for the first time. But when I managed to pluck up the courage to talk to a girl that I really fancied (Yvonne Carter, for example) and hand her a toffee, she rejected me completely with a tirade of abuse. This was in front of everyone in the school. I was deeply embarrassed, and this could have put me off girls for good; thankfully it didn't, although I think it knocked me back a couple of years. It was my mates in the first place who encouraged me to approach Yvonne Carter; now my so–called friends were laughing uncontrollably. I decided right then to give girls a miss, at least for the foreseeable future. I had a good think at home after this thoroughly embarrassing episode and decided Yvonne spurned me because of my appearance. I was poor and I was scruffy, with virtually all my clothes being hand–me–downs and not fitting properly: I did look a bit like Charlie Chaplin. Well, perhaps that is a little far–fetched: probably more like Oliver Twist. But I wasn't begging for more food: I was offering a sweet to a pretty girl and was shot down in cold blood. The reason Yvonne rejected me was probably because I was scruffy. She was an only child and her parents were relatively well off: they had money to dress her well. All siblings wore hand–me–downs from time to time, and it was no fun going to school in a Japanese admiral's uniform.

What this young boy did learn from that exchange with Yvonne Carter was that it would be taboo for a poor person at that time to try and socialise with people with money. When I was older, I looked back and realised that rejection was my first experience of the class system which was in operation then and of course to some extent carries on to this day.

My family was poor, but even at times of depravation the community atmosphere was much better than what it is today. There were decent and kind folk round every corner; they would help you without being asked. But I could never understand why some Catholics and Protestants were always at loggerheads verbally with one another when I was young (although that was before the real trouble started). I was brought up a Presbyterian but was never anti–Catholic. How could I be? Most of my friends were Catholic.

Nowadays I am a vociferous opponent of religious intolerance. There were two camps in Northern Ireland: Catholic and Protestant. Our parents told us stories of the civil war in Ireland, and of course if you were Protestant it was those bloody Fenians who started it all, and if you were Catholic it was the Protestants who were to blame. Nothing has changed much in the world really: we're all into the blame game.

"Why are you fucking drinking with those Fenian bastards, Ken?"

Those were the words that greeted me from Ted Wilson, a Protestant who I had previously met when I first joined the Merchant Navy about five years before. I had travelled quite extensively in those five years and I presume Ted had done the same, but he had still brought all this hatred with him. This greeting directed at me from Ted happened at the bar of the NAFFI in Bridgenorth when I had just joined the Royal Air Force. I was drinking with a couple of lads from Southern Ireland and Ted didn't like that at all. It didn't bother me or the company I was with, but what did bother me was the hatred in Ted's voice and the fact that he was still a bigot after all these years. I put all this hatred down to generations of segregated schools in Northern Ireland; today some schools are mixing and accepting Catholics and Protestants: and not before time.

Every school in Northern Ireland should be open to all religions: then and only then will we fully tolerate each other's point of view and beliefs. Whoever or whatever you think is right or wrong, everything is a matter of opinion, and we all have the right to one of those.

TWO

Tradesmen

My Mother, in her role as a housewife, had five essential and important men in her life: the coal man, the milkman, the pop man, the pastry man and the bin man. These five men were crucial to almost every housewife in post–war Britain, and their trades are almost extinct today, which is very sad: after all, you can't have a chat with a supermarket. Can you imagine a couple in their brand new house being invaded by a bin man? Nowadays it would seem surreal and bizarre to have someone come into your sparkling clean lounge and dump a sack full of coal on the floor, yet that happened when I was a lad.

These huge men had to be strong to carry up to a hundredweight of coal over their shoulder. I remember when I was a boy the door to our little living room being prised open, and this massive man wearing a filthy jacket and trousers, his flat cap tilted to one side, almost covering a face blackened with coal dust, entering our room. In our lounge we had a coal cellar; it was on the wall which was next to the stairs in the hall. This coal cellar had a door which was about five foot high and the cellar itself ran under the stairs; it really was a black hole. That poor man would have to stoop down low to discharge his hundredweight of coal, and his back must have given him permanent pain. That was our little black hole: not in space but right in the middle of our little lounge and home to many families of mice. The coalman provided an essential service to every family: his coal kept us warm in winter.

The milkman delivered our milk, cream and buttermilk, and like all the other tradesmen he would have a natter with any housewife that was up early enough to catch him. There would always be a milkman around when I was on my way to school, and if I had missed my piece of toast because I was late for school, my friends and I would wait until he turned his back and swiftly grab a bottle of breakfast off his van. The pastry man was another important daily visitor. We called him the pastry man, though in fact he was the baker, a purveyor of fine bread and cakes. He would have quite a large van which would have five or six long drawers which would slide out revealing all kinds of freshly baked bread and pastries. When the baker turned into our street he would park round about the middle and all the housewives would converge on the van to put their orders in. The reason the baker would park in the middle of the street and let everyone come to him was economics. The baker had started parking outside each house, but every time he would turn his back to chat to a customer and take her order, myself and a few other lads would quickly be helping ourselves to his pastries. By the time he had got to the end of the street, half his stock would be missing. So after a couple of weeks of this and near bankruptcy, every baker that came to our street from then on would park at a given spot and let the housewives come to him; he would never leave his van.

The pop man was another casualty. He carried every flavour of soft drink that you could imagine and the kids really looked forward to his arrival on the street. The trouble is that he only came once a week, usually on a Saturday, and of course he suffered the same fate as his fellow tradesmen: theft on a grand scale. So of course he followed the same pattern, and instead of individual house calls would stand by his van and let the customers come to him. All good things come to an end, but we kids filled our hats when we had half an opportunity.

The dustbin man didn't deliver food or drink but he still played an important role in our community. These chaps would take anything away for you. Every one of them was tremendously strong, and they had to be: the bins were metal and heavy when empty and you can imagine how heavy they were when full.

Nowadays bins are plastic with wheels; a strong child could wheel them the short distance to the truck. It says on my bin "no hot ashes" and most people put their rubbish in plastic bags, then put them in the bin, and with that you have a nice clean bin. No such luxury for the bygone bin men; they had to contend with everything. There were no plastic bags for a start: everything went into those metal bins from dog muck to hot ashes. But it was carried out with a smile: emptying dirty, smelly and extremely heavy bins to carrying naughty boys who were running from school back home to their mother.

These tradesmen actually enjoyed their work and it was a vocation for them: they had no desire to become rich and they were never in so much of a hurry that they would never find time to chat with you. They enjoyed talking to people as they travelled from street emptying bins and selling their wares.

Housewives enjoyed a diversion from their mundane chores and a chance to have a chinwag. But people talked to each other all the time and, when the tradesmen left the street, women would stay chatting to each other: it was an excuse for a good old natter. Nowadays you can live next door to someone for years and never really know them. That is why these tradesmen were essential and important: when they pulled up in your street, apart from providing a service, they brought everyone out talking to each other.

Supermarkets have all but put paid to that and they are responsible for the demise of many small businesses. That is why these people were important to us: they were part of the social fabric of our community. Is it not a pity that we seem to have lost all that?

THREE

The Gloves

Meet the gang: Jerry Wilson, Sean Connolly, Sean McGee, Billy McCann and me. Except for Jerry and me, the rest were Catholics. As soon as school was out we were free to travel all over Belfast. We were not a gang as gangs go: we didn't go out looking for other gangs to fight. We just enjoyed ourselves, our freedom, and got into a little mischief now and again. More often than not we only came together when one of us had a scam going that we wanted to share, although most of the time Billy and I knocked about in each other's company.

I would walk in front; the rest of the gang would walk in a line behind me as we passed the greengrocers shop with all its fruit displayed outside. I would grab a piece of fruit, and briskly walk on; the next in line would do the same. When the last lad had completed his task we would all scatter like rats up a drainpipe and meet minutes later at a predetermined meeting place and share our spoils. This stealing of fruit only took five seconds maximum. We would do this all through summer at different shops all over Belfast; it was a different shop every time.

Anthony Haughey lived opposite me in our street and he always wanted to be part of our gang. Anthony was a mummy's boy and told tales, but I told him that if he wanted to be part of the gang, then he would have to run errands for us. I would give him money to buy a bag of sweets for me; Anthony would come back an hour later from a journey that should normally take five minutes with a nearly empty bag. He would apologise and say some big lads had robbed him. I overlooked that one; of course, I knew that he had eaten the sweets. A couple of days later I sent Anthony for a bag of apples, and gave him sixpence (that was a quite a bit of money in those days.) This time he came back with a half empty bag and no change, so I smacked him. He ran straight to his Ma who ran straight to my Ma.

My Ma would then say he's a thief, his Ma would deny that, to which my Ma would retort: 'Let me get the boxing gloves out and your Anthony can have a fair fight with Kenny.' Of course, he didn't want to know. But my Ma knew that that would stop the arguing, and they would beat a hasty retreat back into their house. We never did let Anthony into our gang.

The gloves to which my Ma alluded had been in our house for years; I think my Da had bought them second–hand. My brother Fred was a handy boxer and had been encouraged by my Da, so boxing was a big thing in our family. When I was about eleven years old my Da brought me down to White City boxing club.

Henry Hunter who lived near us and was a friend of the family, was the Ulster Amateur boxing champion and boxed out of the White City, so my Da asked him if he would look after me and teach me to box, and so Henry set about teaching me the noble art of boxing. He taught me how to punch, how to avoid punches, how to skip, and sparred with me; in short, he taught me all he knew, and I became quite a handy boxer and enjoyed it tremendously.

I would set off two or three nights a week to train, and of course this was a legitimate way to have late nights. Start off at about six thirty, and back home around ten o'clock.

When there were arguments in the street (and there frequently were), my Ma would get the boxing gloves out. This at the time seemed to me to be a fair way to resolve disputes; on reflection, it wasn't, because I had an unfair advantage over most lads because of my boxing skills. We often had friendly boxing matches in our street; nothing too rough, just honing our skills and messing about most of the time, and besides no one wanted to land head first on the concrete. The other consideration was that if you wanted to retain your reputation as a handy boxer, you didn't want a serious fight with someone who was a better exponent of the art than you were.

Lots of lads went to boxing clubs in those days and there were a few good boxers around. Danny Matthews was one of them; he was extremely handy with his fists. He was about four years older than me and three stones heavier: he should have been a good example to kids, but he was the exact opposite. Danny should never have been taught how to box: he was a nasty piece of work and a bully. From the moment you put the gloves on to box with him, your life was in peril. Nobody boxed twice with Danny if they survived the first time, and if you had a modicum of sense you would avoid him forever. As soon as the gloves were laced up, Danny came at you like a bull: no niceties, just an overwhelming urge to draw blood as quickly as possible. If you were still standing after twenty seconds, you would leg it into your house as quickly as possible before he tried to kill you. Yes, Danny was avoided by everyone. All he lived for was to injure as many people as he could.

I think that's why my friends never took up boxing: watching Danny in action with a pair of gloves on probably put them right off the notion. Danny was dangerously unbalanced, but thankfully he was an exception to the rule and a rarity in the world of boxing: he was treated as an outsider and was never allowed to join a boxing club, so when people eventually got wise to Danny, he got tired of looking for victims and threw his gloves away.

I turned to boxing to learn to defend myself; it was that simple: I wanted to feel reasonably safe. But boxing did much more for me: it made me feel good about myself, it gave me responsibility and esteem, and it is worth bearing in mind that it teaches young men the importance of fighting by fair means, not foul. The gloves are a part of Belfast that I could never leave behind, and which always stayed with me.

FOUR
Deception

When I was a kid, ten, eleven, I would knock at Mrs McKee's door. If someone answered, I would ask if Willy could come out to play; if no one answered the door, I would walk in... In those days doors were never locked, burglars were a scarcity, and anyway where I lived there was nothing to pinch; but more importantly, people trusted each other.

So I would walk into Mrs. McKee's house, go straight over to the fireplace, and help myself to the few pence that were always there on the top beside the clock. Straight to the sweetie shop and fill my pockets with sweets; but I was shrewd enough to finish them before I got home, otherwise questions would be asked of how I could afford sweets.

Questions were already being asked by my older brother because Mrs McKee had started to notice after my fourth appearance in her house –uninvited– that money seemed to be disappearing mysteriously. Well, my brother gave me an accusing look which left me in no doubt that if I valued my health, then the thieving would stop. The thieving did stop, because as well as the threat of injury to my body, my conscience was beginning to prick; so another source was needed for my sweet supply. Necessity breeds invention, calls for desperate measures, so a cunning plan was devised by myself, Billy McCann and Jerry Wilson.

The Rydene Sweet Shop was on the Antrim Road just a couple of hundred yards from my house. It was our favourite because it had the best stock of all our favourite sweets. Mr Jenkins and his daughter Mona owned and ran the shop. Mona was a spinster of about forty years, and her father looked and acted, to our young eyes anyway, to be about ninety years old. His eyesight was very poor, the lens in his glasses were very thick; we observed him on numerous occasions, serving in the shop, putting a customer's money right up to his eyes to make out the value of the money that he was presented with. But this impediment didn't bother him too much: he was too fond of making money. Mona told everyone who cared to listen that her old man would never retire. He would work until he dropped; well, that was good news to our ears. The old man was essential to our plans; in fact, without him there was no plan.

If this plan that we were about to put into operation worked, we would be the cleverest, most cunning and daring criminals of all time: the world's greatest forgers. For our plan to work we had to make sure that the old man Jenkins was serving in the shop, and that his daughter Mona was elsewhere, preferably out of the vicinity. We had two coins that we could work with: an old penny piece and a halfpenny piece. This was decades before decimalisation arrived. The old halfpenny piece was the same size as the silver shilling, which was obviously worth a lot more and would buy a few toffees. The old penny piece was the same size as the silver half–crown, which was far more valuable again, and a few of these in our pockets would give us an endless supply of sweets, fruit and ice cream. When we were not in school, we were out most of the time and we didn't come running home for something to eat every five minutes, so we supplemented our three meals a day with mostly fruit. A lot of times we would skip our cereal or piece of toast in the morning, so we shoved fruit and ice cream down our throats when we could afford it.

Time to put the plan into action. All three of us managed to get an old penny and halfpenny each which we were going to cover in silver paper. Simple you may think; yes, but highly effective as we were soon to discover. Jerry Wilson was the skilled technician in this scheme of ours; what he would do with the help of his Da was to cover the coins with just enough silver paper and rub gently with great patience and skill so as to produce a half–crown and a shilling out of each old penny and halfpenny. Jerry and his Da had an obvious talent for this deception and achieved it with such delicacy that it was difficult for a well–sighted person to tell the difference between our forgery and the real thing, and almost impossible for old Jenkins to see any difference. As far as old Jenkins was concerned, if he could see the sovereign's head on the coin covered with silver paper, it was the real thing. We had to make sure Mona was out of the shop before putting our plan into operation. This wasn't going to be too difficult, as Mona went shopping two or three times a week for food and supplies for the shop, as we observed. She would leave at about ten and arrive back usually about twelve, and that was usually on a Wednesday and Friday, so that was sorted.

We decided that only one of us would go into the shop at a time: two or three of us would cause suspicion. We were about to launch our master plan and we didn't want to jeopardise our mission by upsetting old Jenkins. He became very feisty and irritated at the slightest excuse; he hated kids and the slightest reason would be enough for him to chuck us out of his shop. So Wednesday came, Mona went, and enter myself. I was carrying a half–crown; a forgery of course, and in pristine condition. I have to point out that the old penny was usually slightly thinner than the half–crown, so although old Jenkins might not notice the difference, we couldn't take that chance. Jerry Wilson and his Da resolved that difference in width by packing the old penny to the same thickness as the half–crown with special paper and glue and a bit of filing. The end result was ingenious and undetectable by the shopkeeper.

The time had come to put our long term plan into action; with my stomach churning, I placed my fake half–crown coin on the counter (old Jenkins wouldn't serve a kid until he saw money on the counter first). I asked for three highland toffee bars, twenty fruit salad chews and a quarter pound of brandy balls. He held the coin up to the light and saw the silver sovereign regally looking at him. This would give me ten old pence in change, not to mention the sweets, if he accepted the forgery. And accept it he did, with gusto, much to my great relief and delight: my underpants were dry. Jenkins was miserly and lived for nothing but money. The old boy gave me a silver sixpence and a three penny piece in change; the boys couldn't believe it when I came out of the shop with two pockets bulging of sweets and a tidy bit of change. We divided our illegal spoils and we had decided that if the half–crown went down well, we wouldn't push our luck with the shilling, and anyway Jenkins would wonder where we had acquired this sudden wealth. We had gotten away with it, and had a treasure of sweets to share with my fellow crooks.

This scam carried on throughout the summer holidays. We did not go into the shop every day, although we were tempted; each of us would go in on alternate Wednesdays and Fridays so as not to arouse suspicion, and of course these were the days that Mona disappeared for a couple of hours. We had made quite a bit of money in the change that we had made from the forgeries. The reason we decided to stop one day and not push our luck anymore was because, as we were about to enter the shop with another fake coin, a police car pulled up outside. So we aborted our mission. What it was there for we had no idea; perhaps nervous Mona had noticed something untoward; there might have been a robbery; the policemen might have just stopped by to purchase cigarettes. Our young imaginations were conjuring up all sorts of reasons. But one thing the three of us were certain of was that we were shitting ourselves, and we decided there and then that the scam was to end.

We had made quite a bit of money which Billy had been hiding in his house for us to use when we needed it. I didn't hold on to the money because of the Mrs. McKee incident. Mona was shrewd and probably did notice discrepancies; a simple stock take would have divulged shortages. We had pushed our luck long enough, and anyway a meeting with the RUC wouldn't have made our day or year.

The money we had made through the summer kept us in sweets, fruit, pokes and sliders for weeks afterwards.

FIVE

The Other Side of Our Street

Our street was made up of thirteen two–up two–down houses and one much bigger detached house which was owned and occupied by Aunt Hessie and Uncle George. Their house had three large bedrooms, a large entrance hall, a lounge and large kitchen. Compared to the rest of us in the street, they were wealthy.

They owned two shops: a clothes shop and a sweet shop. Uncle George's son George ran the sweet shop, while Aunt Hessie served in the clothes shop. George ran the sweet shop through the week because Uncle George had a full time job in the shipyard. Both shops were beside each other and situated on the New Lodge Road just a few yards across the road from our street.

In our street, girls were playing hopscotch and skipping; boys were playing handball and kicking balls: all the activities associated with streets the length and breadth of post–war Britain.

At the top of our street, adjacent to the New Lodge Road and standing opposite each other, there was a greengrocer and fruiterers' shop, and the Favourite Bar. There was a lot going on here: a little concrete street with its own public bar and greengrocer shop. A very busy little street indeed, especially when you add to that busy hive a population of about forty one children: there was always something going on.

Summer was the best time: three or four months of no more huddling around the little coal fire at home, especially when you shared it with six other people. The hot weather meant an early start for our gang: after breakfast we would meet to plan the days' activities.

My mother also must have looked forward to the summer months: after breakfast she would be rid of the kids for at least some of the time until early evening. We would be out all day so we would bring some bread butter and sugar sandwiches with us and perhaps an apple or banana. Drinks were no problem: we would follow the milkman, wait for an opportunity and help ourselves from the back of his float: myself, Billy McCann, Sean Connolly, Sean McGee, Jerry Wilson and sometimes Anthony Haughey, even though we didn't trust him too much because of the episode with the errands. But we did tolerate him, as we reckoned that he just couldn't help himself in spite of a good smack from time to time.

Sean McGee, who lived next door to me, joined our little gang occasionally. I was the indisputable leader of our gang: I made the decisions, what to nick, where to go and what games to play. I didn't even have a deputy to take the pressure off me; they were blissfully happy being led.

With a little more intuition, industry or ambition Billy would have been my trusted lieutenant. Billy, like the rest of our gang, was streetwise long before that term became fashionable; survival was the name of the game.

Billy was my most loyal friend; a simple soul, Billy was one of those rare human beings that you could never dislike or take umbrage with. But arse from elbow was often a mystery for my friend Billy.

I remember one summer morning, Billy and I were kicking a ball to each other in my street outside my house when we heard this tremendous bellowing. We looked around and stared incredulously at this big RUC officer (they were all big in those days). We were terrified of policemen; we respected them, as one never argued with a gun or a baton. He shouted 'STOP! STAY!' at the top of his voice (just like he was training a couple of pups) from the top of the street but he was on us as quick as a flash. He brought us to both our mothers in turn and told them that the next time we would be up in court.

My mother retorted: 'What! For kicking a ball?'

'We have had a few complaints missus, of broken doors and broken windows.'

Now I could understand this, because our footballs were not the light, plastic balls that kids kick or head today. For a start we couldn't afford to buy balls of any shape or form; no, we made our footballs. We got loads of newspapers, wet the paper, compressed it, moulded it until we had a proper sized football, let it dry and then bound it with sticky tape.

The end result was a large spherical shaped ball which must have weighed half a stone, and when these balls were kicked by a big bruiser like my mate Billy or psycho Danny Matthews, a window had no chance.

I saw Matthews on a few occasions hit a ball against a closed door and the force of his kick plus the weight of the ball would force it open and leave a dent in the process.

Let me give you a rundown of the families on the other side of our street, Singleton Street.

First off, because of seniority and theirs being the first house, we'll start with Mr and Mrs O'Neill, both well into their late seventies; a lovely, gentle old couple that never bothered a soul. They had a daughter who we saw only once.

When Mrs O'Neill died, Mr O'Neill was heartbroken and distraught, and died himself of a broken heart one month after burying his beloved wife. When I was older, I thought about these two lovely people now and then; what a romance that must have been.

Next to them was the O'Hagan family: they were really destitute (the mice used to leave crumbs at their door). But I never saw Mr or Mrs O'Hagan unhappy. They were always smiling and joking and their kids were the same: their mother and father's happy disposition must have rubbed off on them. The family just travelled through adversity and poverty with a permanent smile on their faces. What a lesson to us all.

Next up were Mr and Mrs Haughey and their brood of three; again they were not bad people, although it was a well known fact that Mr Haughey was an IRA sympathiser. Of course, this was

Anthony's mum and dad; Anthony you will remember was my errand boy, the thief. I know that Mr. Haughey had never done a day's work.

His party piece was to shake hands with everyone: he had a little device in his hand which he hid with his thumb and when you shook hands with him it gave you a hell of a shock. He only ever caught people once, except for Billy who he caught every time. Tricking people with his little device gave Haughey perverse pleasure for years, and, of course, Billy!

The Lanaghan family lived next door to the Haughey family; they had three kids. Their eldest Sean was always arguing with someone, which always led to squabbles between neighbours. Mrs Lanaghan had an argument almost daily and with every family in the street.

'My children don't eat margarine, they eat good country butter on their bread,' she would shout so the whole street could hear, every time she had an argument with someone.

Lanaghan was one of those people that had to argue with someone, anyone would do. You have met the type: never happy or content. If she had lived in a mansion with a bank full of gold, this would not have made any difference; she loved conflict, strife and annoying her neighbours. We had the original bloody neighbour from hell and she lived in our street.

During or after every fight or squabble, she would drag her poor, petrified husband Eugene into the arena, despite his failed attempts to find a new hiding place in the house every time his wife did start a fight.

Eugene really wanted nothing to do with this nonsense, but he didn't really have a choice: he was completely dominated by a bigger stronger woman.

For some reason unknown to me the neighbours had given Eugene the nickname Lucozade, maybe because of a combination of his fast walk, agitated motions and nervous reactions. I always thought that this was unfair, because Eugene was a nice man, although completely under the thumb.

The McKee's were their neighbours, with five kids, four girls and a boy. We never saw much of them at all: the four girls and their brother were mixed up in Irish dancing and seemed to spend any spare time they had practising this pastime.

Mrs McKee you will recall was the woman who had a bad habit of leaving loose change on her mantelpiece to tempt little thieves like me to steal from her, and I gave into temptation, took the money and ran. I often thought about this over the years and always felt guilty. I shouldn't have picked this woman to steal from: they were nice people who minded their own business and didn't bother anybody, but then that fact wouldn't deter a determined thief. They were a relatively prosperous family: Mr McKee had the builder's yard next to their house. He collected scrap and did a bit of building work, so they were relatively well off.

One summers' day us kids were playing in the street when in the midst of us this big black car appeared. We had never seen a car up this close, and it was owned and driven by Dan McKee. He spent the rest of the day giving us kids in turn a ride in his car.

This was a spontaneous gesture by Dan McKee, a man that I had only ever seen once in our street and who I never saw again: after that he became a virtual recluse.

Next to the builders' yard lived my Aunt Hessie and Uncle George. Before I go any further I will tell the sad story about Uncle George.

On his fiftieth birthday, he went for his annual check–up at the Mater Hospital on the Crumlin Road beside the Belfast Crumlin Road Jail. This jail and court combination building was often on the television news in years to come after the Troubles began. Uncle George arrived back at his house after he had been given a clean bill of health at the hospital. Walking into the lounge of his home, he was in high spirits (as you are when your doctor gives you a clean bill of health, thinking that you are invincible). He was surprised by his siblings, who started singing 'Happy Birthday', my mother included, and presented him with a huge birthday cake. This did please him, but he sat down on his favourite armchair, had a cardiac arrest and promptly died. One never knows!

Hessie and George had two kids, George and May; they were much older than the other kids on the street. May wouldn't talk or play with anyone; she was a snob from the cot and remained a snob in later years. George, her brother, was the exact opposite: approachable and friendly. He loved to play cricket and football with the kids when he had time, which wasn't very often. Most of his hours and days were spent in his dad's shop, working from seven in the morning until eight or nine at night, Monday to Saturday.

Sunday was when Uncle George performed in the shop, and that's where all my uncles and my Da congregated on the Sunday morning discussing everything from politics to the price of cigarettes.

Putting the world to right is how they saw themselves, ambassadors of peace and common sense, and never a swear word was spoken. But it was comfortable listening; it was easy listening. Uncle George paid me fifteen old shillings a week (this was good money) to deliver *The Belfast Telegraph* on an evening, and helping cousin George deliver the Sunday papers. I enjoyed the work: I was eleven or twelve, it was my first paying job and this time I was making the money honestly. So I spent a lot of my Sunday mornings after the paper round listening to adult conversations while waiting for my pay for the week's work.

This money was handy for my mother, but the bribe wasn't enough to get me out of going to Sunday school, which I enjoyed at first but eventually began to dislike intensely.

I did not dislike Sunday school as such, but I believe that this was because of a few snobs who attended the church. One or two of them looked at you like you were something dirty that they had just caught on their shoes, and although my mother tried her best to keep my little old suit, which I wore to church, in reasonable condition, she was fighting a losing battle. It was shabby and shiny and fraying at the edges. I was becoming acutely aware of my wardrobe or rather a lack of it. Another reason why I was resentful was because I was the only one in my family being sent to Sunday school, which seemed a tad unfair to me. But I knew that my mother had given up with the others and I was her ray of shining light, and so there was always a good side to going to church.

When I arrived back to the house it was just in time for tea and my Ma made sure I had plenty to eat on that occasion, to the exclusion of the other non–believers.

Well we are getting near the top of the other side of our street. The house beside my uncle George is the Baron household, a grand name for a horrible family; no, I tell a lie: only part of the Baron family was horrible. There was the mother Angela, two daughters Eva and Anna, and one son, called Billy. Now Mrs Baron and her two daughters were salt of the earth, law–abiding citizens who went about their business and never had a cross word with anyone on the street. The rotten apple in the barrel was Billy: he was at least six years older than most of us kids, so invariably Billy being Billy, he enjoyed bullying and teasing the kids. He didn't bother with anyone his age: that wasn't his style, because they would hit him back. Billy was just a disagreeable little shit: he could not see a single day out without making trouble for someone.

His father had fled the roost years before and Mrs Baron could not control her son anymore, so she put her energy into raising her two daughters and let her son get on with it. She regretfully knew that he was a lost cause, and the whole street knew that was why her old man had done a runner.

Billy smacked all of us kids in turn, no exceptions, but I remember one summer he smacked me just for the fun of it, just for looking at him. That was an error of judgement on Billy's part. It wasn't a hard smack, but painful enough for me to tell my eldest brother, Fred. My brother came storming out of the house straightaway, just before Billy could reach the safety of his house. My brother promptly knocked the shit out of him. Billy got the shit knocked out of him on several occasions by older brothers and dads, but he was a persistent bully, so Jerry, Sean, Billy McCann and I decided enough was enough.

Billy's reputation as a bully was bad enough, but it could not surpass his cold–hearted ability to kill or maim any animal that wandered into the sights of his sling. Billy was infamously known as the catapult killer, a title he richly deserved, and birds were his favourite target. I don't think a day went by where he didn't try to injure an animal. Billy had several slings, made every catapult himself, and believe me Billy was an expert marksman. He never missed anything that he deliberately aimed for. Billy's favourite vantage point was his bedroom window. No one could see him up there, his private place. The adults probably didn't know much about his shooting practice, and he wasn't stupid: quite the opposite, he was a cunning little bastard, but we kids knew his vantage point, for on occasions he would invite us to watch while he went about his grisly schemes. So my mates and I decided to set the little psycho up!

One summer morning we walked about half a mile to the nearest R.U.C. station and decided to tell the desk sergeant our story. We brightened up his morning and his colleagues as they gathered round. They humoured us at first, not certain whether to believe us or not. Let's face it: four ragamuffins early on a summer morning telling these hardened coppers about a rat killer on the loose, and willing to rat on one of their own.

At first they found it hard to swallow: this was a first for the R.U.C. But tongue in cheek, and trying hard not to double up with laughter, they decided to go along with our plan. The reason they decided to go along with our little story was the sergeant's decision, and the reason for that was because he knew my uncle George, and uncle George wasn't very fond of Billy who lived next door to him.

The plan was to pass our street every day for five days Monday to Friday in an unmarked police car and in plain clothes. They would park at the bottom of the street for approximately ten or fifteen minutes each day; if nothing untoward happened in the five days, they wouldn't waste any more time on it. We were sworn to secrecy, and it was all very exciting. Sean, Jerry, Billy McCann and I decided there and then that when we became adults we were going to join the police force and become detectives and go on covert operations.

We found out later from the police, that in Shandon Street, the street next to mine, there had been complaints from a man who raced pigeons that a few of his birds were missing, and that and only that was the reason for the sergeant's decision to go along with our story. Anyway, Monday to Thursday passed by without a sign of Billy the sling-shot slayer. That's it then, we told ourselves. Did Billy get hold of our betrayal? He couldn't have: only our gang knew of the plan, and there certainly would not have been a leak from us. We resigned ourselves to the fact that our plan was dashed; four days, no sign of the bird slayer, one more day left, and desperation was setting in.

Friday was about to dawn: this was our last chance. Please make an appearance Billy Baron. We all crossed our fingers... It worked: at about ten o' clock Friday morning Billy opened his bedroom window slightly. Now all we needed were the police to appear. It wasn't a brilliant plan really: the police were arriving at different times every day, but perhaps it was fate for arrive they did at the time Billy was opening his window. We hoped that we were about to catch a pigeon killer. We kids could never figure out how come when birds did appear in our street they seemed to follow a path straight to Billy Baron's house and nowhere else. What we did discover on close inspection after this episode was bird seed on the pavement beside Billy Baron's house, and that was how the crafty bugger always lured the dozy birds.

I of course should have known from the very start that the pigeons did belong to Mr Billy Reid from Shandon Street: his back yard joined our back yard, and anyway there was no one else we knew in the near vicinity who kept racing pigeons.

They were a pain in the arse with their constant warbling: I used to sit on top of our back yard wall and see and hear the noisy, filthy things, when Billy Reid sent them off racing, and the neighbours wished the bloody birds would get lost or emigrate. Yes these birds were a menace as well as a health risk, so perhaps to some of his neighbours because of this Billy Baron wasn't vilified the way perhaps he should have been.

There were a good half dozen pigeons in Billy's sling shot sights now, and as they were oblivious to anything or anyone around them, were feverishly pecking away at the food.

As the birds were dining and Billy was stretching his slingshot to fire, the police arrived; Billy fired... one dead bird one injured bird. Window slammed down, Billy retreats into his bedroom without even noticing that the police had seen everything. The police knock the door, Mrs Baron answers... a few quick words and up the stairs they go to retrieve a very shocked Billy. Out the two officers come with a crying, trembling killer and his mother, in front of a street full of nosey neighbours. The police had told us to keep the whole operation secret, but they didn't think that we would and we didn't disappoint them as we told everyone in great detail about forthcoming proceedings. Billy was held in custody for two hours before being allowed home with his mother. His mother was told to bring him before the courts a week later, the following Friday. They didn't hang about in those days: get it sorted before it disappears from peoples' minds.

Billy was sent down for three months and just escaped a flogging with the birch which was one of the forms of punishment in Northern Ireland. His mother being a quiet private person was utterly ashamed and embarrassed. Billy had been a thorn in his mother's side as long as anyone could remember, and he was a complete opposite to his two siblings; a world apart.

As soon as Billy's mother arrived home she was out apologising to everyone on the street for her wayward son's behaviour, but more than one neighbour thought that they saw a look of relief on her face: a rest from her troublesome son for a few weeks. Of course everyone in our street followed this episode closely, and it was featured in the *Belfast Telegraph* and the *Belfast Newsletter* the following day. His mother had to borrow money to pay a hefty fine. She told my mother afterwards that she had been tormented and humiliated far too long by her son and when he came out of jail she would tell him to leave home. Billy Baron came out of jail after serving the full three months, spent a night at home and was sent packing the next day by a relieved mother. We never saw him again after that, but we heard that he had met a girl who took no nonsense, sorted him out, got him a job and married him; and he did eventually keep in touch with his mother and sisters.

The last stop and at the top of our street was the Favourite Bar. It was a favourite water hole for all the streets running up and down the New Lodge Road. *Why to this day I will never know; but we will leave the pub for another chapter.*

About the Author

Author Kenneth Patterson was born in Crumlin, a village in County Antrim in Northern Ireland in 1942; his father was in the Air Force at the time, and stationed at nearby Aldergrove.

The family moved to Belfast at the end of the Second World War in 1945, into a little two–up two–down terraced house in the New Lodge Road area of Belfast; it was this area and community that would shape his early memories as he grew up with his two brothers and two sisters.

Ken spent some of his working life with both the Merchant Navy and the RAF, having initially started out as a bellboy, then a trainee chef in the kitchens of the Grand Central Hotel in Belfast, acknowledged as one of the finest hotels in Ireland in its heyday; sadly, its doors closed for the last time in 1971.

Today, married with a son and daughter and living in Gloucestershire, Ken is currently working on a third book recalling his experiences in the RAF, a life that took him far beyond the shores of Northern Ireland.

Another Time
Another Place
By Shirley Gault

She was visibly shaken. Angus her dearest friend was in love with her! She really did love him too, but not in a romantic way, more as a brother. Oh no, please do not let this be happening, she thought.

'**Another Time Another Place**' is the first published collection of short stories from the author of the much praised books of poetry, '**Reflections**' & '**Reflections Two.**'

The collection includes '**The Warder's Daughter,**' an autobiographical account, dedicated to the memory of her loving parents, Mary and Albert, which focuses on the dilemmas and delights of growing up in Belfast in the 1960s.

"My inspiration can come from a single word or a beautiful sunset; nature's inspiration is endless," says Shirley, who was born in Belfast and educated at Carr's Glen Primary and Belfast Royal Academy.

Trying Times
By Janice Donnelly

This is an enlightening and touching story of how you can still come out smiling despite all the trials and tribulations of life.

Take Cassie; she is holding down three jobs to make ends meet. Then there is Jo; she is struggling with university and part time work, while friend, Gail, faces up to the prospects of redundancy.

Meanwhile, young and beautiful Orla appears to have it all, but appearances are deceptive. And with his sixtieth birthday looming, Benny and his wife Deirdre are looking forward to a new found freedom, until a phone call changes all that.

This is a multi-layered contemporary tale that will sometimes bring a smile to your face and other times a tear to your eye. Set in a Northern Ireland that is finally at peace – well, almost – *Trying Times* focuses on the strength and importance of relationships in difficult circumstances, taking up where the author's well received debut novel *Buying Time* left off...

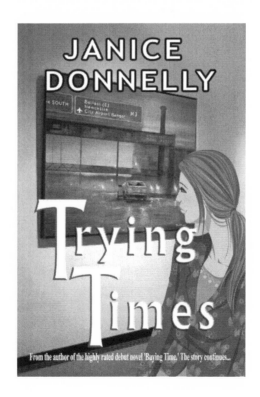

Of Broken Things
By Lynda Tavakoli

It is 1920's Ireland and John Flynn is ten years old when his much longed for sister Stela is born at their isolated cottage. She is a beautiful child whom John sees as a gift sent to alleviate the harshness of his life with an alcoholic father Redmond.

Within a few weeks of Stela's arrival John is unexpectedly left to look after his mother and sister during a snowstorm after Redmond fails to return from one of his many prolonged absences. Stela grows strong under the protection and deep love of her brother but when she approaches her third birthday she inexplicably withdraws from the world. Unforeseen tragedy follows and slowly a web of deceit begins to unravel.

This is a story of divided loyalties and deception, of fear and mistrust, but also one of love and joy that will pull at the heartstrings until the very last page.

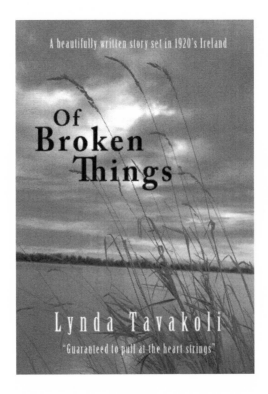

Printed in Great Britain
by Amazon